Come, Thou long-expected Jesus,

Born to set Thy people free;

From our fears and sins release us,

Let us find our rest in Thee.

Charles Wesley

For Sherry and Bob:

Thank you for your kindness and support. May God bless and keep you!

Paul

2/4/20

Testimonials

Cantrell and Seay have provided the Christmas gift we didn't know we were hoping for: an accessible, folksy (in the best sense of the word), thoughtful and vivid explication of why the Word became flesh, and its lively transformative implications for us.

James C. Howell

Senior Pastor of Myers Park United Methodist Church, Charlotte, North Carolina. Author of *Struck from Behind: My Memories of God* and *Why This Jubilee: Advent Reflections on the Songs of the Season*

Wil Cantrell and Paul Seay bring their experienced pastor's hearts and deep knowledge of the Bible and Christian theology to bear on the Christmas story and its meaning for the world, our lives, and the life of faith. What does it mean to follow Jesus in this life? Whether you are a committed Christian, a struggling Christian, or a skeptic, you will find insight into that question in this creative exploration of the meaning of Christmas that expertly weaves history, theology, Biblical knowledge, and personal stories together.

Joseph T. Reiff

Professor of Religion Emory & Henry College and author of *Born of Conviction: White Methodists and Mississippi's Closed Society*

Wil Cantrell and Paul Seay have provided us with a generous Christmas gift! Drawing upon their own personal faith journeys, pastoral sensitivity, and experience, and theological astuteness, they eloquently and passionately communicate the profound meaning and implications of the Incarnation. Individuals and groups will find this short book an inspiring and insightful means of discovering anew 'the reason for the Season.'

Bishop Kenneth L. Carder

Professor Emeritus Duke University Divinity School

Wil Cantrell and Paul Seay have done an amazing job of connecting the new with the old, the current with the ancient. These two pastors honestly address questions of today with solid Biblical and theological insights. Christians and those questioning our faith will both benefit in reading From Heaven to Earth.

Rev. Nathan Malone

Senior Pastor of Christ United Methodist Church, Chattanooga, Tennessee

FROM
HEAVEN
TO
EARTH
Christmas
for New Believers, Old Believers,
and Nonbelievers
Wil Cantrell & Paul Seay

Market
Square
BOOKS

From Heaven To Earth

Christmas for New Believers, Old Believers, and Non-Believers

books@marketsquarebooks.com
P.O. Box 23664 Knoxville, Tennessee 37933

ISBN:978-1-950899-01-2
Paperback Version
Library of Congress: 2019947236

Printed and Bound in the United States of America

Publisher: Kevin Slimp
Editor: Kristin Lighter
Post-Process Editor: Ken Rochelle

Paul Seay photo by Liz Wilson

Unless noted otherwise, Scripture quotations are from:

Dedication

To Monica Hoel,

the guardian angel of

Emory & Henry College,

whose life embodies the spirit

of that great institution.

Table of Contents

FROM HEAVEN TO EARTH

Preface

A good friend of ours was appointed to serve as an associate pastor at a large church right after he graduated from seminary. With his heart and mind filled to overflowing after three years of theological education, he was eager to preach and share all that he had learned. He soon realized, however, that his preaching opportunities would be mostly limited to the Sunday night worship service, which regularly drew far fewer people than the thousand-plus who came on Sunday mornings.

When the time came for his first sermon, he did not let the meager size of the anticipated crowd damper his enthusiasm for the task at hand. He worked tirelessly to include every profound thought about theology or the Bible he had ever encountered into a twenty-minute message. Shortly before the service started, he received a phone call informing him a young member of the church had died suddenly in an accident. That evening over two hundred people, about ten times more than the usual Sunday night crowd, crammed into the chapel. The young pastor realized no one in the stunned congregation had come out that evening in hopes of being dazzled by his brilliance and wit. They needed words other than the ones he had prepared. So, he left his sermon notes in his office.

He began his message by saying, "What happened today has left everyone speechless, including me. So, I was wondering, can we just talk about Jesus?" He went on to share with them what Jesus meant to him. Mostly he read from Jesus' own words in the Gospels along with the declarations of the Apostle Paul about Jesus' victory over death and some of the prophecies of Isaiah that have come to be associated with Jesus. He shared from his own broken heart about the difference he believed Jesus could make in times of loss and confusion. He simply talked about Jesus.

That's our goal in this book. We want to talk about Jesus. We don't want to complain about the commercialism of Christmas or the ways in which Christ is being taken out of Christmas. We know that many people want a war on Christmas, but we come in peace. So much talk about Christmas has come from combative voices. What we want is a conversation, not a bare-knuckle brawl. We are not angry at you or anyone in particular. The rhetoric in recent years about a so-called war on Christmas has only further entrenched two sides of the American cultural divide, and we don't want to add to that.

Nor do we want to focus primarily on how misguided the Church has been at certain points in history in its attempts to follow the one whose birth we celebrate at Christmas. To be sure, we have thoughts about these matters. For us, though, it seems that the best way to speak to what we've been missing in our celebration of Christmas is to have deep, sustained conversation about Jesus. Jesus, after all, is the figure at the center of Christmas.

The mission of the church isn't to win a fight but to embody Jesus' message more faithfully. *From Heaven To Earth* is a call to show grace and hospitality to non-believers, and it is also a call for Christians to take a hard look at our lives in light of the Gospel of Jesus Christ.

This is a conversation we are passionate about. We've given our lives to it.

In many ways, the world is often like that jam-packed chapel. Every day there are reminders that things are not as they should be. We don't always know what to say or how to say it. But we are convinced something needs to be said: something that's true, something that heals, something that brings hope, something that gives life.

So, whoever you are and wherever you are as you read these pages, we would like ask you the same question our friend asked his church years ago: "This Christmas, can we just talk about Jesus?"

FROM HEAVEN TO EARTH

Introduction

A couple of years ago, Paul decided at the very last minute that his church should have a float in the community Christmas parade. The only problem was that no one with any decorating or construction skill was available, three hours before the parade, to put together this float. Somehow, he found a man with a pickup truck and flatbed trailer who agreed to drive the parade route. Along with some members of the youth group and church staff, he raided the church's decoration closet for leftovers. They bought a lot of candy to throw to the crowd. And they made signs out of poster board with the name of the church and benign greetings like "God loves you," "Merry Christmas," and "Jesus is the reason for the season." It was the ugliest, most pathetic float ever, and not even in a Charlie Brown sort of way. Yet, the parade goers all seemed to appreciate it (possibly out of pity). They especially cheered the signs about Jesus being the reason for the season. One woman even shouted out, "Hell yeah, he is!" In the Bible belt, where we live, the assumption is that everyone is Christian, as if we're baptized by simply drinking the ground water.

Maybe, though, you are not a believer. Or maybe you have been in church all your life but have started to have your doubts about many, or all, aspects of the Christian faith. Christmas, as a religious holiday (or at least a consumer holiday with distant religious roots), can be a challenge for people with questions. Everyone talks about God. A lot. To question the truth of the Gospel stories can make you feel like Scrooge. Voicing your doubts also puts a bullseye on you, marking you as a candidate for a Scrooge-like conversion.

Our hope is that these pages can be an open door for a safe conversation. We will not hide where our convictions lie. We are lifelong Christians, doing our best to be passionately devoted followers of Jesus. But, as two friends who over the years have hashed out various doubts and questions in many late-night talks, we know the importance of this kind of safe space. This openness doesn't mean that we won't try to challenge you. We want to offer you a robust account of what we believe. You may leave this conversation unconvinced, and we won't be shocked if we don't answer all your questions. That's okay. Our prayer is that writing this book will make us better listeners to you.

Keeping Christ in Christmas: Be careful what you wish for

The problem with the saying "Jesus is the reason for the season" is that it's nostalgic. It does not have the power to change the way we live. We're kidding ourselves if we think that sprinkling this slogan over our normal Christmas practices will convert us. With its scenes, smells, feelings, and habits Christmas is a holistic experience. We shop until we drop. We see the decorations everywhere. We hear the music. We smell the scented candles and the Christmas trees. We dress differently. All of these practices add up to an experience that, while sentimental, is more seasonal than sacred. Jesus is everywhere, but he's silent and seems to make no difference. Maybe we don't want him to. Could it be that secretly we're comfortable with things the way that they are?

So many times at Christmas we tell the same stories the same way to the same people, and we lose the sense of the audacity of the Christmas claims. After fifteen years of pastoral ministry, we find ourselves talking less and less with skeptics who question the Christmas story, who might challenge us to go deeper with our faith. And we have found our conversations about Christmas with other believers becoming shallower.

Perhaps the reason that Christmas has slipped away is that we've failed to see the story as interesting. The implications of the Gospel story go far beyond and are far more interesting than what kinds of gifts you buy and what charities you give to in December. The Incarnation of God in Jesus Christ touches on every facet of our lives.

We hope that you will find something in these pages that will help you see the beauty of heaven all around you here on earth.

CHAPTER ONE

The Best Way to Send a Messsage

It's no secret that fewer Americans believe in God in 2019 than in the 1950's. Nor is it headline news that (in all denominations) church attendance and membership have been declining steadily for over fifty years. Once upon a time, if you wanted to go out to eat, buy beer, or have a soccer tournament on a Sunday, then you were out of luck. Not today. Our society is open for business and pleasure seven days a week.

One word often used for this new reality is "secular." It's meant to describe a culture that seeks meaning apart from any reference to or reliance upon religious faith. And few can argue that American culture is indeed becoming more secular.

Some of what keeps people away from church is not new at all. In our ever more secular context, a plethora of very old questions are piling up on the church's doorstep. We meet lots of people with questions and doubts about the core claims of the Christian faith. Many struggle with what is often called the problem of evil: How can we say that there's a good, all-powerful, and all-knowing God when human trafficking, cancer, and natural disasters happen on his watch? Why do so many innocent people suffer? If creation is a kingdom, we've got some issues with the way the king is ordering his business.

Tragically, church is often a place where doubt is unwelcome and difficult questions are discouraged. Whether intentional or not, we give the impression that no true Christian ever doubts and that we don't care about your questions.

This is unbiblical. The Bible is full of people who question God. We find this throughout Psalms but also in the writings of the Apostle Paul and even on the lips of Jesus himself. Along with the Bible, Christian history gives us numerous examples of deeply devoted saints who had their doubts and questions. As a matter of fact, most of the people the church considers spiritual giants were people who had seasons of serious doubt. Doubt is a part of the journey of faith. Questioning God is an essential part of having a relationship with God. More than one theologian has said that apathy, not doubt, is the biggest threat to faith. If you doubt and it bothers you, then your faith still has a pulse. But if you doubt and you don't care, that can be a sign of spiritual death.

Other people have problems with Christianity and organized religion. They don't see the teachings and example of Jesus making a real difference in the lives of his followers. This outlook sounds a lot like the quote often attributed to Gandhi: "I like your Christ, but I do not like your Christians. Your Christians are so unlike your Christ."

In response, we might want to lift up examples of the saints we know who truly embody the message of the Gospel. Truthfully, though, we know that the accusation of hypocrisy sticks more often than it should. This mistrust of the church comes from somewhere. It's not simply a made-up charge.

One of Jesus' best-known parables is the story of The Good Samaritan (Luke 10:25-37). A traveler is robbed and beaten as he makes the journey from Jerusalem to Jericho. The bandits take everything he has and leave him to die in a ditch beside the road. The unlikely hero of the story is a Samaritan, who has compassion for the man and goes to great lengths to care for him. But in the story the Samaritan is the third person to come to the scene of the crime. First a priest and then a Levite came to the place where the man lay dying in gutter. And they kept on going, unmoved, uninterested, and too busy to be a neighbor to the man in need. The priest and the Levite represent devoted religious people, acceptable people, part of the in-crowd. The story still rings and stings today because too many people know what it's like to be left in the ditch by religious people.

Several years ago, Paul was on his way to visit one of his church members in the hospital. He stopped at the traffic light on a four-lane road a block away from the hospital. As he looked over at the car next to him, he made eye contact with the man in the driver's seat. They exchanged one of those half-waves that you sometimes nervously give to strangers when you realize you both know that you see one another. When the light turned green, traffic started to roll. But the car next to Paul suddenly stalled. The man was obviously trying to start the car back up, but it wouldn't budge. This was before you could assume that everyone had a cell phone and could call for assistance in situations like these. Back then you might need to find a pay phone (ask your parents what that is) or use the phone at a nearby business. It was the middle of the day. The sun was shining. It was not a dangerous situation. Paul could have easily found some way at least to offer help. Instead, like the priest and the Levite, he passed by, leaving his neighbor to struggle there in the middle of the road. He had a hospital visit to make.

A friend of ours was standing on the back porch of his

house in tears. His father had just died suddenly and unexpectedly. The pastor of their church came out to check on him. The young man looked at his pastor and asked, "Can we pray?" The pastor said, "No, not now. We'll do that later." The pastor then went back inside to continue talking with the rest of the family. Completely baffled at how God could allow his father's death and at a pastor who wouldn't pray with him, our friend ended up then leaving the church for over twenty-five years.

We do not dispute the claim that the church's failure to faithfully follow Christ and love all people plays a significant role in the increasing number of people who want nothing to do with religion. Neither do we deny our personal culpability for our sometimes feeble and half-hearted attempts to share the love we see in Jesus. We resonate with the prolific early twentieth century English writer G.K. Chesterton who, when asked what was wrong with the world, replied, "I am."

All this talk about the rise of secularism and the missteps of the church make some recent research by the Barna Group intriguing. During the same time period in which belief in God and church participation have plummeted, the belief that Jesus of Nazareth was more than merely human has gone up. That's right. According to Barna, about 8 percent more people believe in the divinity of Jesus now than they did twenty years ago.[1]

This, of course, does not mean that nationwide revival is necessarily just around the corner. If anything, it may just mean that Americans are religiously confused. Still, it's striking.

In some ways it is not surprising that people have a higher

---

1 Barna Trends 2018: *What's New and What's Next at the Intersection of Faith and Culture.* Baker Books 2017, 172.

opinion of Jesus than they do of the church or an abstract category like "belief in God." In our experience, people of all faiths and no faith tend to like Jesus immensely. They look at Jesus' life and see beauty, hope, and love in an intensity that's hard to find anywhere else. And, increasingly, even if they have problems with understanding how there could be a God, when they look at Jesus, they see something sacred, maybe even divine.

Who is Jesus? What (almost) everyone can agree on about Jesus

Very few people dispute the fact that a man known as Jesus of Nazareth actually lived in the first century A.D. Every now and then an extreme skeptic tries to make the case that Jesus is simply a fictional character who never lived. Most serious historians and scholars, though, even the non-religious ones, believe Jesus was a real person who walked on this earth long ago. Not all scholars believe in the miracles of Jesus or in his resurrection. Yet, there is a lot about Jesus that they affirm. Here's a list of what (almost) everyone can agree on about Jesus:

- Jesus was a Jewish man from northern Palestine.
- Jesus was born during the reign of Caesar Augustus and Herod the Great.
- Jesus died during the reign of Tiberius and while Pontius Pilate was governor of Judea.
- Jesus died by crucifixion.
- Jesus had a relatively small band of followers, both men and women, who believed that he had been raised from the dead.

- This small group (Christians) grew through the ministry of people like the Apostle Paul.
- Christianity received the acceptance and endorsement of the Roman Empire under Constantine almost 300 years after Jesus' death.
- In 2019, Christianity has more adherents than any other religion in the world.

These are the essential facts of Jesus' ministry in the early 30's A.D. and their global impact. Yet, they do not tell the whole story.

The "Jesus that everyone agrees on" is fascinating. He's the most significant religious figure ever to live, and arguably the most influential person in history. It costs nothing to acknowledge this Jesus of scholarly and historical consensus. It's academically acceptable. It's socially respectable. No one will laugh you out of a bar in a university town for affirming the things about Jesus listed above.

The Jesus who is

The heart of the Christian faith, though, is not "Jesus was" but rather "Jesus is." Ever since his tomb was found empty, Jesus' followers have stubbornly insisted on speaking of him in the present tense. Before they believe a set of abstract principles, or arrive at a philosophical or theological position, Christians are those who have been encountered by the "Jesus who is."

We are not down on doctrine or opposed to theology - not at all. It's just that we don't believe that people come to Jesus first and foremost because of a compelling intellectual argument. People come to Jesus because Jesus comes to us.

One of the problems in American Christianity today is that

many of us prefer the "Jesus we can all agree on," the one who intrigues us, the one who maybe occasionally inspires us, but asks very little of us. Jesus is safer when he's interesting and confined to history. The "Jesus who was" stays quiet while you do the talking. What did he say about giving your possessions to the poor or loving your enemies? Don't worry, that was a long time ago. Keep your money (you earned it, after all). Keep on dreaming of revenge (your enemy deserves it, after all). Your life can remain your own.

But the "Jesus who is" will wake you up in the middle of the night. He will repossess your possessions. He will call you to love people you don't want to love. The "Jesus who was" will not bother you, but the "Jesus who is" will cause you some trouble because the "Jesus who is" has an agenda: to reclaim the world and to reclaim you.

Incarnation

The Gospel of John gives the briefest summary of the Christmas story and yet the fullest statement of its cosmic significance.

John 1:14 says "And the Word became flesh and dwelt among us." That's the entire Christmas story according to John. No wise men. No shepherds. No virgin birth. No manger. If John knew of the birth stories found in Matthew and Luke, he chose not to retell them. For John, this great affirmation is sufficient.

John's cosmic declaration comes in the opening, or prologue, of his Gospel.[2] The prologue in John is a poetic account of God's activity in the world through the Word.

2 John 1:1-18.

In the beginning was the Word, and the Word was with God, and the Word was God. He was with God in the beginning. Through him all things were made; without him nothing was made that has been made. In him was life, and that life was the light of all mankind. The light shines in the darkness, and the darkness has not overcome it... He was in the world, and though the world was made through him, the world did not recognize him.

John 1:1-5, 10

What John shows in these verses, which have been called the Hymn to the Word, is that Jesus is not some kind of alien visitor to the world, even though he comes from heaven. As the Word that was with God in the beginning, Jesus has been intimately involved in every aspect of God's work in creating. His coming to earth is a homecoming. The King of Creation comes to reclaim his kingdom.

Christians call this belief that Jesus is God's Word made flesh the Incarnation. Incarnation literally means "enfleshment." This doctrine is at the heart of the church's teaching that Jesus is fully divine and fully human. Yet, it is not a scientific statement, meaning that it's not something that you can analyze under a microscope. It's more mystery than mathematics.[3] You sing about it more than you explain it.[4]

3 If you spend much time with math, though, you find that, like science, it involves a great deal more mystery than we often associate with it.

4 Theologians have written a lot on the meaning of the Incarnation. Some of it is very good, and we hope that you will investigate it further. Don't let the abstract language and theological vocabulary discourage you. God is worthy of our most rigorous thinking. Academic theology gets unwarranted criticism for being unnecessarily complex. The problem is not that theologians engage in technical, specialized conversations but rather when professional theologians talk only among themselves, leaving out other academic disciplines and especially people in the pews. But before we criticize, we should note that pastors and churches are guilty of practicing

Wrap it in a person

When we were attending Emory & Henry College, our chaplain, Rev. David St. Clair, would often say that, "the best way to send a message is to wrap it in a person." It makes sense. What's more effective:

- A sign that says "Welcome to our church" or a greeter whose job it is to show hospitality to newcomers?
- A note that says, "Thinking of you on your wedding day" or worshiping at the wedding with the bride and groom as their families unite and then dancing the night away at the reception?
- Saying, "We'll pray for you while you're in the hospital" or going to visit, walking their dog, and taking care of their family during their stay?

The Incarnation means a lot of things. We could fill several libraries with all that has been written about this doctrine, but one way of understanding the Incarnation is to say that Jesus is everything we need from God wrapped in a person.

About two months into our first year of seminary, as we were busily making new friends and keeping up with the demands of our studies, a phone call from Paul's father interrupted everything. Paul's mother had been battling cancer for several years, and the treatments could no longer stop the spread of the disease. She was in her last days. This was the phone call to come home. Paul purchased a plane ticket and threw a bunch of clothes in suitcase. Wil drove him to

---

the faith while socially insulated from life outside Christian circles.

the airport and then began calling friends and making travel arrangements for everyone so they could be there in person for their friend.

After his mother's death, many people expressed their love and support for Paul and his family. One of them was Jeff, whom Paul barely knew at the time. Jeff was on staff at the church where Paul's dad served as pastor. He came with a small group of people to bring dinner to the family a couple of days after the funeral. They didn't stay long. Before walking out the door, Jeff unexpectedly threw his arms around Paul in a giant bear hug. If Jeff said anything, Paul doesn't remember it. But Jeff's action said what needed saying. Over a thousand people consoled the family in one way or another during those days. Almost twenty years later, the cards and letters are stored in a box. Sadly, most of the emails are gone. But Paul's memory of Jeff's embrace continues to speak those words of comfort. He embodied the community's collective message: we are here for you.

Christmas celebrates the Incarnation. God comes from heaven to earth for us and embraces the whole world in the person of Jesus Christ.

CHAPTER TWO

Why Do I Need a Savior?

You may have noticed a bumper sticker that began appearing a few years ago: "Not All Who Wander Are Lost."[5] Or, perhaps you have someone in your family who proudly wears a T-shirt with this slogan to Christmas dinner as a silent protest against the church-going sensibilities of other family members. The message is not so subtly aimed at Christians, cautioning them against labeling those outside the church as "lost." It's a helpful reminder, actually. What often looks to some like being lost can often be, for the pilgrim, the path to God and deeper faith. The slogan reminds us of other art forms and artists who push back against Christianity's apparent claims of certitude and exclusivity. The song "Closer to Fine" by the Indigo Girls is beautiful in its defiance.

For years, one of the fastest-growing religious categories in America has been the so-called "spiritual, but not religious" group. Many thoughtful people are open to the idea that there may be something "more" out there and that spirituality is a good thing (maybe not a God-thing, but a good thing). Their

---

5 These words may well come originally from J.R.R. Tolkien, a writer who saw no incongruity between imagination and Christian faith.

objection to Christianity has to do with the question of who's in and who's out.

Consider the difficult questions raised by the lives of many people from cultures across the globe who have never given Jesus much thought, but live long and happy lives. They are often highly ethical, good people. If there is an afterlife, and if Jesus came to save us so that we can spend eternity in heaven, then what about those wholesome ethical people who aren't Christian? And what about all the people who lived before Jesus was born? What happened to them?

Of course, there are bad people who need a dramatic intervention to keep them from harming others and completely wasting their own lives, but don't those people really just need quality mental health care? Even if they need a savior of some kind, we might argue that, because we are sober and successful, we don't need saving in the same way that they do.

This leads us to another criticism of Christian teachings on salvation, from what at first seems like a very different perspective. We'll call it the American objection. Our culture believes that self-sufficiency is the goal of life. Most of our heroes are those whom we would call "self-made." From this perspective, Christian talk about sin, brokenness, and the need for salvation is nonsense at best, and offensive at worst. Christianity is big on admitting weakness. And if there's one thing that Americans are allergic to, it's weakness.

Then, there are the theological objections. If humanity had reached such a state that we could only be saved by God becoming human and giving his life for us, what does this say about God's ability as creator? Shouldn't God have done a better job creating the world in the first place so that such a painful intervention would not be necessary? And does this salvation through Jesus really work? Does it make any difference in the world? It sure looks like the world is still very much unsaved.

These are important questions. Anyone who thinks that they have easy answers to these and other objections to matters at the heart of the faith should think again. As Christians we do well to listen to such questions, and we dismiss them at our own peril.

We do not pretend to be able to answer these questions to everyone's satisfaction. But we hope that taking a fresh look at the language of sin and salvation in the Bible can open doors both for the skeptic and for the Christian.

Jesus as Savior

The first explicit reference to Jesus' saving purpose in the New Testament comes in the opening chapter of Matthew when an angel appears to Joseph in a dream. Joseph has just decided to end his engagement to Mary after learning that she is expecting a child that is not his. God intervenes through this messenger and tells Joseph that the child in Mary's womb is from the Holy Spirit.

> ***She will give birth to a son, and you are to give him the name Jesus, because he will save his people from their sins.***
>
> **Matthew 1:21**

The angel doesn't take time to give a definition of sin or how exactly Jesus would save his people from their sins. It's important to remember that the Bible isn't a dictionary or an encyclopedia. Though that would be much more convenient, wouldn't it? Sometimes it would be nice to be able to use the Bible as a quick-reference: just flip it open to "S" for sin, read a brief definition, close the book, and get on with your day. Instead, when you come across something complex like sin, very often the Bible keeps moving. If you want to learn more about what it means, the Bible invites you to read on, and immerse yourself in the story.

What is sin?

That's a huge question. Unfortunately, Christians often settle for small answers.

One day Paul was talking with a friend who is not a Christian. She expressed confusion, really frustration, at the idea of sin. "I just can't imagine," she said, "calling bad things I do 'sin.' I might call them mistakes or flaws, but sin? I don't get it."

Though she has plenty of Christian friends, and she has attended worship services several times, it's not hard to see how she could think that Christians believe that sin is synonymous with bad deeds or mistakes. That's the extent of how we often speak of sin.

A lot of Christian talk about sin can be summarized something like this: "Sins are the bad things we do that separate us from God." This definition of sin has some truth to it. Still it's incomplete and more than a little misleading. Sin, from this perspective, becomes primarily about breaking the rules, and overcoming sin simply means keeping the rules Let's take some time to fill in our understanding of sin.

First, sin is a God-thing

Sin is about God. That may sound like an odd thing to say. What we mean, though, is that we cannot know what sin is without God. Sin is the story of humanity's broken relationship with God, our rejection of God, and refusal to live with God. Perhaps the biggest problem with defining sin primarily as rule-breaking is that it puts humanity at the center of the story. The story then becomes more about us than about God. Sin is something we do, and it's something that we need to avoid. This approach implies that God is distant at best. It's as if God is an absentee landlord who leaves a set of regulations for us to follow while he's away. God puts his expectations in a sealed envelope and goes back to his far away home.

In a sense, you could say that too much Christian talk about sin is essentially atheistic. We make the mistakes, and we'll fix them. We're the problem and we're the cure. Leave God out of your definition of sin and you're likely to leave God out of the solution.

Second, sin is our condition

Sin isn't merely something that we do. Sin is a condition. Our sinful actions are symptomatic of a deeper ailment. The angel didn't say that Jesus will help his people improve their flaws. Mary's child will save his people, liberate them from their sins. Sin is a state that requires not willpower but rescue. It's not that we're slightly lost and can find our way if given a map. Nor do we have a sickness that can be treated with a home-remedy. Sinners don't just need assistance. We need saving.

The Apostle Paul speaks of sin in terms of slavery, especially in Romans:

- For sin shall not be your master... **(Romans 6:14)**
- ...you used to be slaves to sin... **(Romans 6:17)**
- When you were slaves to sin... **(Romans 6:20)**
- But now that you have been set free from sin... **(Romans 6:22).**

As a Pharisee steeped in Hebrew Scripture (what Christians call the Old Testament), the story of the Exodus would have loomed largely in the background for the Apostle Paul. Any talk about slavery would have called to mind the slavery of God's people in Egypt. They were slaves to Pharaoh, and later on in the wilderness they discover that they are slaves to themselves. The Israelites were unable to free themselves from Egypt and unable to find their own way through the wilderness to the promised land. Their only hope was God's intervention.

The Apostle takes us inside this slavery to sin in Romans, chapter 7. Here he demonstrates why we cannot simply use our own willpower to walk away from sin.

> ***So I find this law at work: When I want to do what is good, evil is right there with me. For in my inner being I delight in God's law, but I see another law at work in the members of my body, waging war against the war of my mind and making me a prisoner of the law of sin at work within my members. What a wretched man I am! Who will rescue me from this body of death?***
>
> **Romans 7:21-24**

One of the most apt analogies for the power of sin is addiction. With addiction, the human will is broken. A person with a serious addiction wants to be free and at the same time is unable not to want what's killing them.[6] Similarly, Christian tradition speaks of sin as the brokenness of the human will. In the grip of sin, humanity longs for healing but at the same time desires the things that bring destruction.

Third, sin is communal

American Christians tend to speak and think of sin in individualistic ways. This isn't surprising given that we live in a radically individualistic culture. We are conditioned to be primarily concerned with our own individual wants, needs, and concerns over and against those of the whole. Our starting point for reflection on most any issue is first and foremost individual. Corporate or communal elements are an afterthought.

So, well-meaning people often ask questions like, "Is it a sin if I order ice water and then fill my cup with a soft drink?" (If it's not a sin, it's at least dishonest and tacky.) Or, "Is it a sin if I tell a little white lie?" It's not that these sorts of questions are unimportant. Rather, the problem is that too much Christian reflection is done as if we're wearing blinders. The only thing that matters in this conversation is my individual sin. This is to limit sin and to underestimate its terrible power.

In the Bible, the language of sin is corporate. Sin is the shared state of the human family. The Israelites were captives together under Pharaoh, held in bondage as a people. Sin is communal because it destroys true community. When we see the human family abusing or neglecting each other,

---

6 We certainly do not mean that people who struggle with addiction are somehow worse sinners than the rest of us. Quite the opposite. People in recovery and AA are examples for the rest of us about what it means to stop living in denial of the power of sin in our lives. And just as all have sinned, we all have certain compulsions and habits that intrude upon the life that God has for us.

we see sin at work. We were created by God for community, and in this sense, sin keeps us from being fully human.

Racism, xenophobia, and greed are not sins that an individual simply wakes up one day and decides to commit. As middle-class, white American males we (Paul and Wil) aren't always racist, greedy, or fearful of others just because we want to be. Most of the time we really want to do better. It's in those moments where we strive to live more lovingly and justly that we realize the extent to which we, along with other privileged people like ourselves, are caught up in a sinful way of being that we can't simply discard like a piece of clothing. Sin sticks to us. It forms (or deforms) humanity into a kind of anti-community, where we harm and neglect one another.

A definition of sin

With all this in mind, we suggest this definition of sin: *Sin is an enslaving power that disrupts, derails, and distorts our relationship with God, others, and ourselves. And sin is a master that we humans learn to serve willingly.*

Sin as Missing the Mark

Because sin so thoroughly disrupts human life, it causes us to miss God's purpose for humanity. The Greek word for sin used in Matthew 1:21 and throughout the New Testament is *hamartia*. This word actually doesn't mean evil deeds or wickedness. It's an archery term that means to miss the mark. Interpreting sin as missing the mark provides a much broader understanding of sin than simply doing bad things which separate us from God. Missing the mark implies humanity was created with a purpose to fulfill rather than to simply avoid doing bad things.

To sin is to settle for a purpose other than the purpose for which you were created and designed. It is to orient your life in such a way you miss the whole reason for living, to trade a glorious eternal destiny for a few cheap thrills here on earth. Sometimes sin involves doing morally bankrupt, hurtful things and sometimes sin is simply choosing to pursue a shallow purpose with our lives.

Hollywood produces approximately five hundred movies a year. These movies represent all sorts of genres from romantic comedies to mockumentaries. In recent years, however, the top-grossing movies come from two very closely related genres: princess movies and superhero movies. Why do these genres do so well? Because they are all about fulfilling your life's purpose, your destiny. Every princess has a destiny to rule a kingdom and every superhero has a destiny to use their superpower to combat evil. Something deep within us is attracted to the idea of destiny.

The Bible is full of stories of people fulfilling their destiny or sometimes tragically shirking it. Abraham, against all odds, became the father of many nations. Moses led the Hebrew people out of slavery in Egypt. King David restored the faltering monarchy. Esther saved the Jews in Persia from certain peril. Jonah was running from his destiny to take the message of God's love and grace to the people of Nineveh until spending a little time in the belly of a big fish got him straightened out. An overzealous Pharisee who held Roman citizenship named Saul became the perfect person to share the good news of the grace of Jesus Christ with the Gentile world.

When we see sin as missing the mark or missing the glorious destiny to which God calls each of us rather than just breaking the rules, suddenly it becomes clear why we all need to be saved. We need to be saved because we were not created for a life captive to sin, which misses God's goal for us. We were created to love God and love each other.

What is salvation?

This is another huge question to which Christians are guilty of giving a small answer. Just as we too often think of sin in individualistic ways, we let individualism dominate our thinking on salvation. We also tend to think of salvation almost exclusively in terms of what happens to us when we die. Salvation for Christians has become escapism, fire insurance for the afterlife. It's become a way for Christians to avoid many of the Gospel's claims on life in this world. Like we did in our earlier conversation about sin, it will be helpful to broaden our vision of God's salvation.

Salvation: journeying toward the promised land

Let's look back to the first chapter of Matthew, where the angel visits Joseph. There's a clue to the meaning of salvation in the name of the one who will be born to save. The name that the angel tells Joseph to give his adopted son is transliterated from Greek into English as Jesus. His Hebrew name is Joshua, which means "God saves."

In the Old Testament, Joshua is the one who leads God's people from the wilderness, where they've wandered for forty years, to the land promised by God. They first entered the wilderness as fugitive slaves from Egypt. God's purpose for Israel was not for them to live as slaves or to stay lost in the desert. Through the first Joshua, God saved the people from slavery and restored them to their destiniy: to dwell in the land and to make the one true God known to the world. The new Joshua, Jesus, also came to help his people fulfill their destiny.

Angel touchdown: Salvation and Luke's Christmas story

Luke's account of Jesus' birth tells us about an angel speaking of God's saving purpose in Jesus. The heavenly messenger appears to the shepherds and says,

> ***Today in the town of David a Savior has been born to you; he is Christ the Lord.***
>
> **Luke 2:11**

There is an overlooked detail in this unforgettable scene that is illuminating. It's not just what the angel says but how (or where) the angel says it.

You probably have a picture that comes to mind when this story is told, one that's highly informed by Christmas cards and children's pageants. Perhaps you envision a group of shepherds dressed in some kind of a cross between a toga and a bathrobe looking up in the sky and listening to the heavenly messenger. Where else would the angel be besides hovering just below the clouds? Isn't that where angels belong? Most Christian art places the angel in the air above the shepherds. And there's nothing in many of our best-known English translations to make us see it any other way.

> ***An angel of the Lord appeared to them, and the glory of the Lord shone around them....***
>
> **Luke 2:9**

...the angel of the Lord came upon them, and glory of the Lord shone round about them....

Luke 2:9 (KJV)

Two Shepherds and an Angel by Kuroda Seiki, Kuroda Kinenkan, Tokyo National Museum, Japan.

We assume that the angel appeared in the sky. Yet, the Greek reads a little differently. It can be translated,

An angel of the Lord stood in front of them.

Authors' Translation

Instead of floating in the air, the angel announces the good news with feet planted on the earth. The heavenly messenger didn't simply do a fly over. The good news wasn't air-dropped in. It was delivered face-to-face by an angel who stood on the same ground as the shepherds.

That's quite different from our conventional ways of imagining this scene.

The good news (gospel) of the Savior's birth, the salvation he was born to bring, is *from* heaven but it's not only *for* heaven. It's for this world. Salvation doesn't float up in the air or just wait for you in the next life. Salvation is a way of living in this life, where your feet touch the ground.

Christians have become obsessed with heaven and the afterlife. This causes us to limit our understanding of Jesus as our savior. His saving becomes only about getting us to heaven. It's as if the main problem is that we need a ride and Jesus drives the bus that gets us to heaven.

Who's in and who's out?

The two of us have known each other most of our lives. We were roommates in college and in seminary. About half way through our freshman year of college, our world was rocked by questions that had never really occurred to us in high school: "What about people of other faiths who live their whole lives without ever hearing about Jesus? Will they spend eternity separated from God?" Questions like these kept us up at night.

On the one hand, it seemed cruel to believe that God could reject someone who never had a chance to hear the Gospel. It struck us as narrow and exclusive. Would the merciful God who meets us in Jesus really punish someone for eternity? What about a child? What about someone who lived in poverty in the developing world who never had a chance to learn about Christ?

On the other hand, there are difficult implications in giving everyone a "free pass," as it were. If everyone is ultimately "in," is that really fair? Would this mean that the distinctive beliefs of Christianity really don't matter? Is everything relative? And also, what about Adolf Hitler and other terrible people? Will they just walk right into heaven with no questions asked?

We worried at times that these doubts would disqualify us from becoming pastors one day. What kind of future pastor isn't certain about something as basic as the afterlife? It helped us to learn we were hardly the only Christians wrestling with these kinds of questions. One source of comfort was the Apostle Paul himself. In his letter to the Romans, chapters 9 through 11, he wrestles with the disturbing question of whether God has rejected the Jewish people. It was oddly reassuring to see that there was not a quick and easy answer for the Apostle.

While some Christians seem completely confident about who is in heaven and who is in hell (and even their room assignments), the global body of Christ has, over the centuries, offered a variety of answers to these questions about what happens to non-believers when they die. Some have suggested that those who die as unbelievers will get another chance at the final judgment. Others have said that the forgiveness offered in Jesus is so radical that it overcomes humanity's rejection of God.

This conversation is likely the source of the Roman Catholic doctrine of Purgatory as well as the Baptist teaching on the age of accountability. Neither of these terms are found in the Bible. They are attempts at an alternative to a completely cut-and-dried declaration on who's in and who's out.

This is an important conversation. While we don't have all the answers (we can't tell you what the wallpaper in heaven will look like), we have both become more at peace with uncertainty. We have also become more Christ-centered in our reflection on these matters. That is, wherever we land on our provisional answers to these questions, we believe our answers must be based on who Jesus Christ is, and not ever set aside or bracket out the living center of our faith.

As important and interesting as this is, though, there is so much more to the biblical vision of salvation than the afterlife.[7]

Believers want to live forever after they die one day. That's great. Jesus certainly says that whoever believes in him will never die (John 11:25-26). But you don't have to wait. You can live today. The New Testament teaches that the salvation given in Jesus here and now is about dying with Jesus and living in resurrection hope.

---

7 For further reflection on questions about heaven and eternal life we highly recommend N.T. Wright's book, *Surprised by Hope: Rethinking Heaven, the Resurrection, and the Mission of the Church.*

Or don't you know that all of us who were baptized into Christ Jesus were baptized into his death? We were therefore buried with him through baptism in order that, just as Christ was raised from the dead through the glory of the Father, we too may live a new life. If we have been united with him like this in his death, we will certainly also be united with him in his resurrection.

Romans 6:3-5

Then [Jesus] called the crowd to him along with his disciples and said: 'If anyone would come after me, he must deny himself and take up his cross and follow me. For whoever wants to save his life will lose it, but whoever loses his life for me and for the gospel will save it.'

Mark 8:34-35

Back to Luke's Christmas: The Glory of the Lord

Luke says when the angel stood in front of the shepherds the glory of God was present. In the Old Testament, the glory of the Lord is a way of speaking of the very presence of God. God's glory was too much for Moses to look upon in Exodus 3:6 & 33:17- 20. It filled the tabernacle in Exodus 40:34. And in that pasture full of shepherds and sheep near Bethlehem, the glory of the Lord was at eye-level.

Everything about the Christmas story according to Luke tells us that salvation is not reserved for the next life. It spills over to flood the present with God's glory and power. Reclaiming Christmas means reclaiming the hope of salvation. We can say with the psalmist, "I am still confident of this: I will see the goodness of the LORD in the land of the living" (Psalm 27: 13).

Angel army

There's one more detail about the angel's announcement to the shepherds that we don't want you to miss. After proclaiming the birth of the savior, Luke says the angel was joined by a plethora of other angels. Most translations call this crowd of angels the "heavenly host." But the word *stratia*, usually translated as host, really means army. Read it again:

> ***Suddenly a great army of heaven's angels appeared with the angel, singing praises to God...***
>
> **Luke 2:13 (GNT)[8]**

Can you see it? Not a choir but an army of angels covering the ground, surrounding the shepherds, shouting, "Glory to God in the highest and on earth peace..." God's message is not just on the lips of the angels but also their feet.

Richard Lischer writes about how Martin Luther King, Jr. would rush to the scene of bombed-out black churches to hold prayer meetings. The KKK did its worst and King would show up and preach while the smoke was still rising. Lischer asked some people who were present what exactly King said in these messages. They didn't remember. But, Lischer says, each of them remembered where King was when he gave his message. Simply showing up and standing in the ashes was its own message.[9]

Jesus was not sent to earth simply to get us out of here. Salvation is not God's plan of evacuation. Salvation is God's invasion.

---

8 Scripture quotations marked (GNT) are from the *Good News Translation in Today's English Version* - Second Edition Copyright © 1992 by American Bible Society. Used by Permission.

9 Lischer, Richard, *The End of Words: The Language of Reconciliation In a Culture of Violence*, Wm. B. Eerdmans Publishing Company 2005.

CHAPTER THREE

Jesus' Family Tree

For many people, Christmas comes with an abundance of family traditions. Maybe you always start decorating for Christmas on the same day each year or the ornaments always go in the same spot on the tree. Perhaps several of those ornaments have special memories attached to them. They were wedding gifts, or for "Baby's First Christmas." At Christmas, lots of families gather around a table and share stories of matriarchs, patriarchs, great aunts and uncles, cousins, and in-laws.

Of course, this idealized picture of family doesn't resonate with everyone. Christmas can also be an awkward time of dealing with family dysfunction. Sometimes members of the same family can't stand each other. Many people only see their family once a year, and that's quite enough.

Recall the defiant and ironic celebration of alcoholism, drug abuse, and self-destruction in the song "Family Tradition" by Hank Williams, Jr. Some of our family and Christmas traditions highlight our brokenness rather than togetherness.

Family can be the greatest blessing we will know in this life, and family can wound us more deeply than anyone else. And sometimes it's just mixed. Even the families that appear to be perfect have their moments when they, too, are pretty messed-up.

Still, whenever possible, there is real value in knowing your family story, even if it's a painful story. In fact, research from the Family Narratives Lab at Emory University has shown that children and adolescents who know their family history exhibit greater levels of maturity and emotional resilience.

Family reminds us that we are a part of a story. Countless people's lives and choices went into making us who we are. This is true whether we're talking about a nurturing family or a destructive family. We all enter this river downstream from those who came before us.

The same is true of Jesus. He didn't come as a stranger from heaven, like an alien visitor. He was born into a family. He entered the river downstream from a great story that had been going on for thousands of years.

Jesus' family tree according to the Gospel of Matthew

Matthew's Gospel begins by showing us how Jesus enters a drama that is already in progress. Christmas, for Matthew, isn't just the story of Jesus' birth but of everything that God has been doing to prepare the world for the arrival of the Messiah.

Matthew then takes the reader on a journey through the history of God's people. This genealogy looks a lot like the lists of patriarchs and descendants that we find in the Old Testament. As we often do with the genealogies of the Old Testament, most modern readers scan or skip entirely this portion of Matthew (and the genealogy of Jesus in Luke 3:23-38).[10]

When trying to read through this family tree, it's easy to get overwhelmed or even lost. It can be helpful to notice that Matthew divides Israel's history into three segments:

1. From Abraham to David **(Matthew 1:2-6)**
2. From David to the exile in Babylon **(Matthew 1:7-11)**
3. From the Exile to the Christ **(Matthew 1:12-16)**.

Let's look at the significance of each of the turning points of Israel's story that Matthew lifts up: Abraham, David, Exile, Christ.

Abraham

Like Matthew, Luke's Gospel also includes a genealogy of Jesus. There are several key differences between Luke's genealogy and Matthew's. Most noticeably, the two genealogies move in opposite directions. Matthew begins with the Old Testament patriarchs and works his way down through time to Jesus. Alternatively, Luke begins with Jesus and works his way back to the Old Testament (you might say that Matthew's genealogy is in descending order while Luke's is ascending).

But arguably the most significant difference is that Luke takes the story all the way back to Adam, the very first human

10 We have chosen to write mostly about Matthew's genealogy in this chapter because Matthew presents his genealogy at the very beginning of his Gospel as part of his telling of the Christmas story. Luke, on the other hand, places his version of Jesus' genealogy later at the beginning of Jesus' public ministry. There is much to be learned from comparing the similarities in these two accounts of Jesus' genealogy and hard historical questions to be asked about the differences. For the purposes of this chapter, however, we are focusing primarily on what we learn about the meaning of the Christmas story from Matthew's account of Jesus' family tree.

being. Matthew only goes as far back in time as Abraham.

This should remind us of the very first words of Matthew's Gospel. Before he takes us on his whirlwind tour of the Old Testament, Matthew introduces Jesus, the main character of his book, in this way:

> ***This is the genealogy of Jesus the Messiah, the son of David, the son of Abraham.***
>
> **Matthew 1:1**

We cannot overstate the significance of Abraham for Israel's story. He can rightly be called the founding father of God's people. In Genesis, we read about God's promise to use Abraham and Sarah to start a new nation:

> ***The LORD had said to Abram, 'Go from your country, your people and your father's household to the land I will show you. I will make you into a great nation, and I will bless you; I will make your name great, and you will be a blessing. I will bless those who bless you, and whoever curses you I will curse; and all peoples on earth will be blessed though you.'***
>
> **Genesis 12:1-3**

Abraham's story marks the beginning of God's people.

David

David was Israel's greatest king. Though, as we will see, he was far from perfect. Israel had more military victories under David than any other king. From the time he is first introduced in 1 Samuel 16, David is portrayed as God's chosen one. God wanted David, not Saul, to be King of Israel. Before David dies God tells him,

Your house and your kingdom will endure forever before me; your throne will be established forever.

2 Samuel 7:16

The idea of David's kingdom will long outlive him. His reign will be the golden age of Israel, and many people will continue to hope for a ruler like David to come and lead God's people.

Exile

If David's reign sometime around 1000 B.C. is the high-point of the Old Testament story of God's people, then the Exile is surely the lowest.[11] The army of a foreign king, Nebuchadnezzar, invaded Judah and, through a series of forced deportations lasting from 597 B.C. – 581 B.C., took many of its inhabitants back to Babylon. The temple was destroyed, and the people understandably wondered whether or not God had abandoned them.

Babylon was later conquered by the Persian Empire, and King Cyrus of Persia began sending the captives back home to Judah around 537 B.C. In the fourth century B.C. Judah fell under the rule of the Egyptian Ptolemaic Dynasty and then the Syrian Empire. After the Maccabean revolt in 167 B.C., the Jews gained relative independence under their own Hasmonean Dynasty. While the Hasmonean Dynasty was marred by division, violence, and civil war, it allowed Judah to once again enjoy political sovereignty for about a hundred years until the Romans invaded in 63 B.C. Jesus was born under Roman rule. His ministry, death, and resurrection took place while his homeland was occupied by the Roman Empire.

---

11 To read more, see 2 Kings 24-25.

Christ

Matthew's genealogy ends with the birth of Jesus. Now the stage is set for the Gospel narrative to begin. Jesus is not just the end of the list. He is the goal, the destination. Jesus is the reason Matthew took us on this journey to begin with. All Scripture has been aiming in this direction since the beginning. Jesus' appearance on the scene is not random. God has been preparing for this moment for a long time.

The four Old Testament women in the genealogy

Most of the people listed by Matthew are kings and patriarchs. Yet, somewhat unusual for his time, Matthew also includes four women from the Old Testament: Tamar, Rahab, Ruth, and Bathsheba.

These are not the women you would expect. It wouldn't have been terribly surprising if Matthew had included Sarah, Rebekah, and Rachel, the wives of the great patriarchs. The only woman in the genealogy whose presence might seem less surprising is Mary, the mother of Jesus. But, as we will see, even Mary's place in this list is also remarkable.

Tamar

The story of Tamar will make you blush. We doubt that it comes up very often in Sunday school, and it is never one of the stories children learn at Vacation Bible School. In the story, Tamar disguises herself and becomes pregnant by her father-in-law, Judah (if you don't believe us, read it for yourself in Genesis 38 - after you put the kids to bed). For centuries, readers have assumed that Tamar seduced Judah, leading to the birth of Perez and Zerah. But upon closer examination it's not so clear. Recent scholarship has questioned whether or not Tamar sought a sexual encounter with Judah or if, like a majority of readers believe, Judah assumed that she did. This raises an uncomfortable but important question: Is this a story of Tamar taking control of her situation or of Judah taking control of Tamar?

Rahab

Rahab was a prostitute and a resident of the city of Jericho. She welcomed the Israelite spies into her home as they prepared for the invasion and conquest of the city. As a result of this hospitality, her life was spared when the army of Israel moved in. We read about her in the book of Joshua. In the New Testament, she is also cited as an example of courageous faith in both in Hebrews and James.

> ***By faith the prostitute Rahab, because she welcomed the spies, was not killed with those who were disobedient.***
>
> **Hebrews 11:31**

> ***...was not even Rahab the prostitute considered righteous for what she did when she gave lodging to the spies and sent them off in a different direction?***
>
> **James 2:25**

Rahab was also a gentile. She feared the God of Israel, and Matthew says that she married an Israelite named Salmon, but it is still odd to find her name recorded here in this genealogy.

Ruth

The Old Testament book of Ruth is the first of only two books of the (Protestant) Bible named for women. The book tells of how Ruth, a gentile, becomes a part of God's people. Her famous words of devotion to her mother-in-law, Naomi, have a lot to say to us about what it means to join God's people through Jesus the Messiah:

> ***Don't urge me to leave you or to turn back from you. Where you go, I will go, and where you stay I will stay. Your people will be my people and your God my God.***
>
> **Ruth 1:16**

Ruth is from Moab, and Deuteronomy 23:3 says that Moabites are banned from the assembly of the LORD. Yet, the book ends by telling us that Ruth, the Moabite, became the grandmother of King David. A Moabite is not supposed to be welcome in the gathering of God's people. But here she is. Ruth the Moabite is in the genealogy of David and Jesus.

The wife of Uriah (Bathsheba)

Matthew never calls her by name. He only calls her the wife of Uriah.

One evening, King David is walking around on the roof of the palace and he sees Bathsheba bathing. Because he is the king, David has the power to send someone to retrieve Bathsheba and bring her back to the palace. David sleeps with Bathsheba and she becomes pregnant. David tries to cover this all up, but when it doesn't go as he planned, he arranges for Bathsheba's husband, Uriah, to be killed. Though their first child dies in infancy, Bathsheba later bears David a son,

Solomon, who later will become king.[12]

There is no way to say with certainty why Matthew chooses to omit Bathsheba's name from his genealogy and refers to her instead as the wife of Uriah. Some scholars believe Matthew did so because he felt Bathsheba was complicit in her affair with David by purposefully violating ancient customs for modesty by intentionally bathing in a location where David could easily see her from the palace, in hopes of being noticed by the king.

Other scholars note David, Israel's king, was the most powerful person in Bathsheba's world." Bathsheba had no official status. And with that great power imbalance it was virtually impossible for Bathsheba to say no. These scholars point out that David's affair with Bathsheba was most likely non-consensual and can rightly be called sexual assault. In their thinking, Matthew refers to Bathsheba as the wife of Uriah to highlight the sinfulness of David forcing himself on another man's wife.

Regardless, Matthew didn't have to include a reference to this deeply troubling episode. Why in the world didn't Matthew just write, "Jesse was the father of King David. David was the father of Solomon. Solomon was the father of Rehoboam?" Just leave out that part about David's affair with Bathsheba. But there it is: "David was the father of Solomon, whose mother was the wife of Uriah."

Why these four women?

For centuries, Christians have proposed different reasons that Matthew may have had for referencing these particular women in his genealogy. Maybe the mention of Tamar and Bathsheba has to do with the unusual circumstances around

12 You can read the story of David and Bathsheba in 2 Samuel 11 & 12.

Mary's pregnancy and Jesus' birth. Is Matthew reminding his readers that this is not the first unplanned or scandalous pregnancy in the history of God's people? Or might the mention of these stories be a kind of warts-and-all picture of Jesus' family and a reminder that God chooses to work through, and in spite of, human imperfection? Others have pointed out that at least two, and maybe all four, of these Old Testament women were gentiles.[13] It is possible that Matthew is sounding the theme that will emerge slowly throughout his Gospel: the inclusion of the gentiles.

We should remember that Matthew's Gospel was originally read aloud communally, not privately. Not only were many people illiterate, it would have been cost prohibitive for everyone in the early church to have their own copy. It's worth imagining what this dynamic might have meant for the scandalous material that Matthew's genealogy alludes to. How did the first listeners react when they heard, "Judah was the father of Perez and Zerah, whose mother was Tamar?" Would the reader have stopped to refresh the congregation on the details of that story? Awkward!

The fifth woman: Mary

The inclusion of Tamar, Rahab, and Bathsheba would have probably made the crowd whisper among themselves a bit. Yet, Matthew saves the most shocking detail for last:

> ***...and Jacob the father of Joseph, the husband of Mary, and Mary was the mother of Jesus who is called the Messiah.***
>
> **Matthew 1:16**

---

13 Rahab and Ruth certainly were gentiles. While 2 Samuel 11 doesn't tell us about Bathsheba's ethnic identity, it does call her husband Uriah the Hittite. So, her husband, though serving in Israel's army, was not a native to Israel. Similarly, we don't know for sure about Tamar, but some have suggested that she was born a Canaanite before marrying into the family of Jacob (Israel).

Joseph is not the father of Jesus. He's not named as the father of anybody. He's the only man in the whole genealogy who is not a father. The whole list is built on the repetition of the phrase "...was the father of...." Here at the very end, like a master composer, Matthew strikes a very different note. Not only is Joseph not the father of Jesus, in dramatic fashion, Matthew isn't going to tell us who is. He ends this portion of the story with that startling sentence. In the beginning of the next section, Matthew will tell us that the Holy Spirit is responsible for Mary's pregnancy. For now, though, he will leave the matter unresolved. What might it have been like to hear this read aloud for the first time? How do you think the crowd reacted to this?

Matthew's main point: Son of God, Son of Abraham

Matthew wants his readers to see Jesus as the fulfillment of the promises to both Abraham and David. In Genesis 12:3, God promises Abraham "all peoples on earth will be blessed through you." And in 2 Samuel 7:16, God promises David: "Your house and your kingdom will endure forever before me; your throne will be established forever."

As the Messiah, Jesus – like David – is God's anointed one whose kingdom will never end. And as with Abraham, through Jesus, God will bless not only the Jews but all the peoples of the earth. The genealogy taps into both of these promises by showing how Jesus is descended from both of these major figures in Israel's Scripture. The genealogy closes with an affirmation of God's overarching plan.

> ***Thus there were fourteen generations in all from Abraham to David, fourteen from David to the exile to Babylon, and fourteen from the exile to the Messiah.***
>
> **(Matthew 1:17)**

Matthew says that each of the three periods of Israel's history spans fourteen generations. The three sets of fourteen (7 x 2) likely symbolize fulfillment and God's guidance of history.[14] The number three is also often symbolic of completion, and the threefold repetition of fourteen generations almost certainly is meant to enhance the sense that all time has been moving toward the arrival of Jesus Christ.

Matthew's second main point

Matthew intentionally brings up surprising and even unseemly parts of Jesus' family story. This is his second main point, and it may be as important as his emphasis on Jesus' Davidic lineage. Jesus family contains outsiders, like Ruth, who blessed Israel and insiders, like David himself, who acted shamefully. Real life is messy, and Jesus was born to be fully human and to live life in the real world.

Many people in today's world believe Jesus does not want anything to do with them until they get their lives cleaned up. This is why people often stay away from church or take a hiatus from daily personal prayer after significant moral failures or otherwise embarrassing episodes in their lives. They think the only way to please God is to live a life in which you never make costly mistakes.

If a quick look at your life reveals evidence of compassion and heroism as well as cowardice and moral debauchery, that makes you exactly like the type of person Jesus loved and called to be his disciples in the first century. If your Christmas celebrations involve family tensions, simmering resent-

---

14 Though some scholars have debated this point, it seems obvious to us that there is significance to the fact that fourteen is a multiple of seven, a number of perfection, and that it recurs three times. Matthew surely did not choose these numbers arbitrarily, especially since, as has been pointed out by others, the first and third sections of this genealogy don't actually contain fourteen generations.

ments, and unhealthy coping mechanisms as well as beautiful expressions of generosity, faith, and love, then your celebrations are exactly the type of Christmas celebrations at which Jesus is likely to appear.

An old-fashioned, Old Testament Christmas

Matthew's story of Christmas and of Jesus begins boldly. These are the first words of the New Testament, and with Matthew's genealogy, the New Testament starts out by looking back at what has come before. This looking back will continue throughout this first Gospel and the rest of the New Testament. The New Testament does not leave the Old Testament behind. The Old Testament, which is so much more than the opening act for Jesus, lives on in the story of Jesus and in the earliest Christian writings (like the letters of the Apostle Paul). The famous line by William Faulkner is appropriate here: "The past is never dead. It's not even past."

Jesus is a part of God's story, not a departure from it. In fact, he's more than just part of the story, he's the goal of the story.

We hope that this discussion of the genealogy at the opening of Matthew's Christmas story has challenged you to think of Jesus in the context of the ongoing story of God's people.

The ongoing story of your life

Before we turn our attention to Jesus and Judaism in chapter 4, we would like to ask you to consider how Jesus might help you understand the story of your life. Just as Jesus' genealogy teaches us that his life must be understood as part of the ongoing story of God's work among God's people, we believe God has been at work in each of our lives long before our first conscience thought.

Sometimes conversion to the Christian faith is presented as an experience through which a person moves from a place devoid of God to a life in which God is fully present. It's true that the difference between someone's former (pre-conversion) life and new life in Christ can be dramatic. But one of the essential affirmations of the Gospel is that we are never without God. We may not acknowledge God, and we may not know how to (or want to) seek God. Even then, God is still with us and at work. Most of the people who come to faith in Jesus through our churches tell us their newfound faith helps them see how God has been present in their lives all along.

John Wesley, the founder of the Methodist movement in eighteenth century England, referred to Jesus' presence in our lives before we personally accept faith for ourselves as prevenient grace (or preparing grace). He believed through Jesus, God's grace was already at work in each person in the world regardless of the degree of their faith or lack thereof.

We hope that you can look back and see how God has been at work throughout your life's journey. God lovingly created you and has called you to a life of discipleship. Jesus' genealogy reminds us that we are part of a much larger story, something bigger than we are. And this means that God is making more of our lives than we ever could on our own.

CHAPTER FOUR
Jesus is Jewish?

Different cultures celebrate Christmas quite differently, and generally, if you do not understand the culture, you will not be able to appreciate the celebration. Wil learned this lesson all too well during his first Christmas celebration with the family of his wife, Rebecca. Wil knew the importance of making a good first impression at the Christmas gathering, so he worked diligently to learn the names of each person expected in attendance. This was no small feat since over forty people often showed up for Christmas breakfast with her mother's side of the family, and nearly the same number attended the celebration for her father's side of the family later in the day.

Upon arriving at the home of Rebecca's paternal grandfather (Papa King) for the afternoon Christmas celebration, Wil quickly realized he had focused largely on names while neglecting to learn the culture of this side of the family well enough. He spent much of the gathering hungry, unable to compliment anyone's cooking because he hadn't eaten any of it yet, until someone informed him there was no set time for the meal. Everyone was free to get food whenever they wanted it. Wil wondered why Papa King looked at the gift Wil had purchased for him and, without opening it, said, "It's just what I had been needing." Wil found the gesture insincere. How could he know if he needed it or not until he unwrapped it? Later, he learned that Papa King used this same phrase as his way of sincerely showing his thanks for every gift he received each year, a practice not unlike saying, "Peace be with you" in church. You say it to everyone because you mean it for everyone.

Most crucially, Wil failed to notice how each member of the family meticulously wadded up and hid away the wrapping paper from each gift they opened. Being self-conscience and not wanting to make a mess, Wil disposed of his left-over wrapping paper in the trash. This meant he was without ammunition in the massive wrapping paper ball fight which took place after all the gifts had been opened (an annual tradition in which old and young alike pelt each other with balls of paper)! He knew the names well enough, but he failed to understand the culture.

In the chapter 3 we discussed the names and back-stories of many of the people in Jesus' family tree. In this chapter, we will discuss the culture of first century Judaism into which Jesus was born because without understanding the first century Jewish culture, it's difficult to fully appreciate the significance of Jesus' birth and later adult ministry.

A history of forgetting

One of the great scandals of modern Christianity is the failure to recognize the Jewishness of Jesus. Generations of otherwise faithful Christians have worshiped, served, and studied in church for their whole lives while barely, if ever, coming into contact with Jesus the Jew.

Once a parishioner told Wil, in all seriousness, "Pastor,

you said in your sermon today that Jesus was a Jew. But we all know that Jesus was a Christian." Similarly, several years ago Paul learned about a young man from the congregation who told his mother-in-law at Sunday dinner, "The preacher said today that Jesus was Jewish. That's a new one. Where did he get that?"

These people are lifelong believers, raised in devout Christian homes. Yet Jesus' Jewishness wasn't handed down to them as one of the basics of the faith. Not only did Jesus live, die, and rise as a Jew, but Jesus' earliest disciples, including the Gospel writers and the Apostle Paul, were Jews. Their belief in Jesus as Messiah didn't nullify their membership in the Jewish family. Believing in Jesus wasn't a way out of Judaism. Christianity began as a movement within Judaism. While there was tension between early Christians and some of the leaders within Judaism, Jewish Christians remained involved in the synagogues until around 70 A.D. after the destruction of the temple. Following Jesus was a way of being faithful to the God who first called Abraham and rescued the Israelites from slavery in Egypt. Judaism is not only the background of the New Testament, it's heritage. Judaism is the atmosphere of the New Testament.

Tragically, Christianity has screened out this essential part of Jesus' identity. Judaism has been reduced to a historical footnote, at best. At our worst, Christians have wrongly portrayed all Jews as enemies of Jesus and the Christian faith. Judaism has been seen as something Jesus, the Apostle Paul, and others had to overcome in order to be who God had called them to be. Yet, without Judaism we have only a partial picture of Jesus. And there are far too many examples of how this willful ignorance has had truly tragic consequences. Let's take a look at what we've been missing.

Why does it matter that Jesus is Jewish?

1. Because it clarifies which God we are we talking about.

A particular God

The ancient world had many gods. As we discussed in chapter 2, Jesus' name in Hebrew (Joshua) means "God saves." And not just any "god." The God to whom Jesus' name bears witness is the God of a particular people and a particular story. This is the God who:

- Creates everything that is (Genesis 1)
- Calls Abraham and Sarah to be parents of a new nation and a new people (Genesis 12)
- Liberates Israel from slavery in Egypt (Exodus 14)
- Speaks to God's people through prophets (Jeremiah 1)
- Goes with Judah into Exile in Babylon (Ezekiel 1)
- Brings the people back from Exile (Ezra 1).

When God calls Moses from the burning bush, God's introductory words are, "I am the God of your father, the God of Abraham, the God of Isaac, and the God of Jacob" (Exodus 3:6). After freeing the Israelites from Pharaoh, God addresses the people at the beginning of the Ten Commandments by saying, "I am the LORD your God, who brought you out of Egypt, out of the land of slavery" (Exodus 20:2). This God has a story that's intertwined with Israel. To forget Jesus' Jewishness is to forget this story and this God.

One God

While the ancient world had lots of gods, the Jews had only one God. Christians, too, believe that there is only one God.

The fact that Christianity is a monotheistic faith (believing in only one God) rather than a polytheistic faith comes from the Jewish faith of Jesus and his earliest followers. When asked to name the greatest commandment in the Law, Jesus went back to Deuteronomy 6:4.

> ***...Hear, O Israel, the Lord is our God, the Lord is one.***
>
> **Mark 12:29**

Christianity's doctrine of the Trinity is rooted in the belief in one God. There is one God who exists eternally in three persons: Father, Son, and Holy Spirit. Trinitarian theology is not a departure from monotheism but rather grows out of it. Without a fierce commitment to the oneness of God, there is no doctrine of the Trinity.

A very different God

The Old Testament witnesses to a God who is very different from the other gods in the Ancient Near East. God is nothing like the gods of the Canaanites, such as Baal, or the many gods worshiped by the people Israel encounters along the way. The LORD is known for being steadfastly committed to Israel, for being characterized by mercy and justice. The God of Israel is mysterious and passionate. One of the most moving passages in the Old Testament is found in Hosea. It reads like a lament for God's beloved but wayward child, Israel.

> ***When Israel was a child, I loved him, and out of Egypt I called my son. But the more they were called, the more they went away from me...my people are determined to turn from me....***
>
> **Hosea 11:1-2a & 7a[15]**

---

15 We highly recommend that you read and study Hosea 11:1-11.

We cut Jesus off from the story and character of this God when we forget that Jesus is a Jew.

2. Because it helps us understand what the title Christ means.

The story of Israel and of the Jewish people is embedded not only in the name Jesus but also in the title Christ. "Christ," which is a Greek word for the Hebrew word "Messiah," means "anointed one." In the Old Testament, a king or a prophet was anointed by God, set aside to minister to God's people. In the years leading up to Jesus' birth, many Jews looked for a new anointed one (Messiah) who could restore what had been lost in exile, years of war, and in Roman occupation. This title, Christ, is so important that as early as the writings of the Apostle Paul, it becomes like a second name for Jesus. In fact, the Apostle often seems to use the name Jesus and the title Christ nearly interchangeably. But the richness of this wonderful title is rendered almost meaningless when we forget that Jesus is a Jew.

3. Because of the inclusion of the Gentiles... outsiders...us.

In Matthew 1:21 the angel says to Joseph, "...you will name him Jesus, for he will save his people from their sins." The people the angel speaks of are Jews. According to Matthew's story, Jesus spends his earthly ministry proclaiming the good news and healing among his own people. In Matthew 10:5-6, Jesus sends the twelve out on a mission to preach, cast out demons, and heal the sick. The mission, at this point, is just for their people. Jesus tells them to go only to "the lost sheep of the house of Israel." Jesus and his disciples keep their work in-house, so to speak, until after his death and resurrection.

But from the very beginning, Matthew's story of Jesus also points to something more: to a time when the outsiders to God's covenant with Israel will be invited in. There are gentiles included in Jesus' genealogy. And when Jesus is born, a star appears in the sky that draws magi (wise men who were non-Jews) to make a pilgrimage to Jerusalem and ultimately to Bethlehem, in search of the newborn King.[16]

This theme reemerges at the close of Matthew's Gospel. In Matthew 28, the risen Jesus meets his disciples on a mountain in Galilee and gives them what has come to be called the great commission:

> ***Go and make disciples of all nations, baptizing them in the name of the Father and of the Son and of the Holy Spirit....***
>
> **Matthew 28:19**

The Greek word for nations is *ethne*, and it's the same word used for "Gentiles." The mission is no longer just in-house. This Gospel is for everyone. Jesus is born to save his people, but not only his people.

The book of Acts is largely about how this messianic movement within Judaism began to draw in Gentile believers. The Apostle Paul's ministry was aimed at bringing the Gospel to the Gentiles, and in Ephesians we read of the beautiful work of God in bringing Jews and Gentiles together in Christ.

> ***For he [Jesus] is our peace, who has made the two groups one and has destroyed the barrier, the dividing wall of hostility...making peace, and in this one body to reconcile both of them [Jew and Gentile] to God through the cross....***
>
> **Ephesians 2:14-16**

---

16 We will have more to say about the wise men and what their coming to worship the king of the Jews might mean in chapter 7.

The majority of Christians in the world fall into the category of Gentile. We do well to remember that we are among the outsiders who have been invited in. This radical message of Gentile inclusion and reconciliation is lost when we forget that Jesus is a Jew.

4. Because we live in a post-Holocaust world

Between 1933 and 1945, six million Jewish women, men, and children were murdered in a government-sponsored genocide called the Holocaust. It began with pogroms and mass-shootings of Jews and culminated in millions of Jews being sent to death camps like Auschwitz and Dachau. By the time World War II ended, nearly two-thirds of the Jewish population of Europe had been killed.

How could an educated Christian nation carry out this sickening campaign of systematic murder? There's no quick answer, but two major factors are rising nationalism and long-nurtured and widely accepted anti-Semitism. The latter relates directly to our topic here. Anti-Semitism was as common and condoned among Protestant Christians in Germany as racist language and behavior in the American South was toward African Americans between the Civil War and the Civil Rights Movement.

It did not help that theology and biblical scholarship of the day did nothing to challenge these prevailing attitudes. In fact, students of theology could find support for anti-Semitic views in the major voices in scholarship like Gerhard Kittel. Kittel was a fervent advocate of the Nazis. He had a history of writings that spoke of Jews as enemies of Christians.[17] Kittel's major work, The Theological Dictionary of the New

17 We recommend the documentary Theologians Under Hitler (Steven Martin) which tells the story of theologians like Kittel as well as Paul Althaus, who was the leading scholar of Martin Luther at the time, and church historian Emanuel Hirsch.

Testament, has been a standard in theological education for decades (even to this day). Christians in Germany were mostly silent, if not active participants, in the Holocaust.

Christian theology has rightly been reckoning with its complicity ever since. Here are some helpful questions we can ask ourselves:

- Do I tend to speak of Judaism (either ancient or modern) negatively?
- How well-informed am I about Jewish history?
- Might I be repeating things I've heard in sermons and Sunday school lessons without ever questioning their accuracy?

What can we do? We must make sure that our statements about Judaism (first-century and modern) are based in fact and not stereotypes. We can show gratitude for the countless ways we are blessed by the fact that Jesus is Jewish. And, we can show respect by learning more about Judaism then and now. This will help us speak respectfully of Jewish people, whether we're talking about Judaism of the first or twenty-first century.

These are just a few of the reasons that it matters that Jesus is Jewish. We could list many more.[18]

What do we mean when we say Israel?

In this book we have been using terms like Israel's history, Israel's God, and Israel's Scripture quite a bit. And the

---

18 If you would like to learn more about this important topic, we recommend works such as *Jesus Through Middle Eastern Eyes* by Kenneth E. Bailey, *Jesus and Judaism* by E.P. Sanders, and *The New Testament and the People of God* by N.T. Wright.

modern nation of Israel is in the news a lot. Does our discussion of Judaism and Israel's history have anything to do with the controversy surrounding modern-day Israel and Palestine? What do we mean by all of this?

When we talk about Israel's history, we generally mean the story of God's people that begins with Abraham in Genesis 12. Genesis 1-11 covers the period before the Patriarchs (Abraham, Isaac, and Jacob), sometimes called primeval history. This is no less a part of the story of God's people, but we link the beginnings of Israel's history with Abraham because of God's promise to start a new nation through him and his wife Sarah. The title Israel comes from the name given to Jacob in Genesis 32:22-32 after Jacob's wrestling match with God (or God's messenger) by the Jabbok River.

This history runs through the reign of David and Solomon, and there we find a fork in the road. After Solomon's reign the kingdom divided, and Israel became the name of the Northern Kingdom, while Judah became the name of the Southern Kingdom. The Northern Kingdom, Israel, was destroyed by the Assyrian Empire. Later, (as we discussed in the previous chapter) the Southern Kingdom fell to Babylon. The difference is that the life and faith of the Southern Kingdom survived the Exile, and Jerusalem, Judah's capital city, was resettled and the temple rebuilt.

The return from Exile marks the beginning of Judaism. Many years later, the terms Jew and Jewish were used for the first time, most likely in reference to the region of Judea in which Jerusalem is located. Judaism grows out of the life and faith of ancient Israel.

In what is often called Early Judaism, Israel became a way of referring to the past and hoping for the future, even though it ceases to refer to a specific nation. Not nearly all

Jews lived in Palestine, and Israel was one way of naming all God's people scattered across the known world.

Israel's God is the God who is constant throughout this story. Christians believe that this is the same God who comes to us in Jesus of Nazareth. Jesus called Israel's God, Father. Several theologians have said that Christians worship the God who freed Israel from Egypt and raised Jesus from the dead.

We sometimes speak of Israel's Scripture instead of the Old Testament or Hebrew Bible. This is because the earliest Christians had only the books that we call the Old Testament. To them, it was not old but simply the Scriptures. We are careful about calling these writings the Hebrew Scriptures because even the Hebrew Bible isn't written entirely in Hebrew.[19] Most likely, the Apostle Paul and others in the early church read the Septuagint, which is a Greek version of our Old Testament.

So, what about modern-day Israel? It's complicated. Strictly speaking, this chapter deals with first century Judaism. As our discussion above about the Holocaust indicates, what we know about the past has implications for the present. And, as we said earlier, the past is never totally in the past. At the risk of greatly oversimplifying a very complex problem, Christians should be on guard against anti-Semitism, which seems to be on the rise, and at the same time we do well to avoid being blindly loyal to any nation, whether our own or modern Israel. No nation is perfect. We remember that Jesus challenged people in his day to love their enemies. His message of peace is as relevant and challenging as ever.

19 Some passages within of the books of Daniel and Ezra were originally written in Aramaic.

What was Judaism like two thousand years ago?

Just as there is great diversity within modern Christianity, with many different denominations across the world, so it is with modern Judaism. We could never say that there is just one version of Judaism any more than we could say it of Christianity. The same was true of Judaism in the first century. Some scholars even talk about Judaisms (plural) instead of a singular Judaism.

One of the most helpful sources outside the New Testament is the first century Jewish historian Flavius Josephus. Josephus' activity took place decades after Jesus' earthly ministry, so his writings may describe his own time better than that of Jesus. Like any author, Josephus had his own agenda and biases. Nevertheless, his work is invaluable for many reasons, not the least of which is how he helps us to see the diversity of belief and practice within first century Judaism. Josephus speaks of four major sects or philosophies within Judaism: the Pharisees, the Sadducees, the Essenes, and the Zealots.[20]

As you may know, the Gospels have a lot to say about the Pharisees and Sadducees. However, their references to the Zealots are sparse. And the word "Essene" is not used in the New Testament.

Pharisees

Josephus tells us that the Pharisees were known for their interpretation of the Jewish law. Of the four groups he mentions, the Pharisees would have been most in touch with the lives of everyday people. It is important to point out that Pharisees were not priests. They were laypeople, not

20 Josephus doesn't actually mention the Zealots by name. Instead he speaks of a fourth major philosophy within Judaism, and the description matches other biblical and historical writings concerning those who were zealous for the law.

clergy, as we often envision them to be. One of their greatest concerns seems to have been helping to make the law accessible to the people.

In the Gospels, Jesus is quite critical of the Pharisees at times. This has led many Christians to make sweeping, and not fully informed, statements about the Pharisees. Sadly, too many of us have transferred this negative association with the Pharisees onto Judaism in general. It is helpful to remember that not all the Pharisees in the Gospels are portrayed as hostile to Jesus. One great example of a Pharisee who was drawn to Jesus is Nicodemus, whom we first meet in the third chapter of John's Gospel. By the end of the Gospel of John, Nicodemus, instead of being an opponent, appears to have become a believer in Jesus. He joins in helping Joseph of Arimathea in preparing Jesus' body for burial (see John 19:38-40).

Sadducees

Much less is known about the Sadducees than the Pharisees. Both Josephus and the Gospels record that the Sadducees did not believe in resurrection or any kind of afterlife (thus the very old preacher joke that they were "sad you see" -- we just said it was an old joke, not a necessarily a good joke).

Some scholars believe that a large number of the Sadducees were priests. However, the portrait given by Josephus makes them out to be secular and opportunistic. In the Gospels, they are lumped together with the Pharisees as opponents of Jesus' ministry. In spite of the unflattering depiction of the Sadducees in both Josephus and the Gospels, Christians should be cautious about claiming to know more than we can about them. And, as with the Pharisees, we must not use this fragmentary knowledge of the Sadducees as a basis for generalizations about all Jews.

Zealots

A Zealot is someone who is passionately devoted (zealous) to a cause or conviction. In the case of Jews in the first century, Zealots were ardent advocates of the Jewish law and temple. One thing, among many, that would have rallied the Zealots was the Roman occupation of Jewish Palestine. Luke's Gospel lists a man named Simon the Zealot as one of Jesus' twelve disciples, though Luke does not tell us what is meant by this label.[21] Many scholars think that Simon was among those committed to overthrowing Rome, even if it meant using violence. Barabbas, a prisoner who was freed by Pontius Pilate instead of Jesus, is not explicitly called a Zealot, but the description of his crime corresponds to the common picture of the Zealots. Mark 15:7 says that Barabbas "was in prison with the insurrectionists who had committed murder in the uprising."

Essenes

The Essenes are described by Josephus as well as the Jewish philosopher Philo (who lived and wrote during the time of Jesus and Paul). The Essenes were separatists who believed that the religious leadership in Jerusalem was hopelessly corrupt. Their solution was to withdraw from larger society into the desert in search of spiritual purity. While the Essenes are not mentioned by name in the Gospels, it is possible that we see their influence in the ministries of both John the Baptist and Jesus.

John the Baptist conducted his ministry in the wilderness and was very critical of the religious establishment. We

21 Like Luke, Matthew and Mark also have lists of the twelve disciples of Jesus. Only Luke calls Simon a Zealot. In an apparent effort to smooth out differences among the three lists, many translations (including the NIV) label Simon as a Zealot in both Matthew 10:4 and Mark 3:18. However, in the Greek, Matthew and Mark call this Simon "the Cananean."

don't know much about Jesus' relationship with John prior to Jesus' own ministry, and each Gospel portrays Jesus and John's knowledge of each other differently, but at the very least we can say that Jesus was sympathetic to John's teaching.[22] Does this mean that Jesus was also influenced by other Essene teachings? We simply do not know for sure. We will have more to say on John the Baptist in our next chapter.

The community at Qumran (Dead Sea Scrolls)

In recent years, many scholars have suggested that the sect that Josephus and Philo call the Essenes may in fact be the community that lived at Qumran and produced what are known as the Dead Sea Scrolls. This seems highly likely, and there are many similarities between the descriptions of the Essenes and the community described by the writings in the Scrolls. The Dead Sea Scrolls, which were only discovered in 1947, have transformed our knowledge of Judaism before and during the time of Jesus. As the name suggests, the Scrolls were found in caves near the Dead Sea. They include more than nine hundred manuscripts of biblical texts, as well as texts that were unique to this community, most of which had never been seen previously by the wider world.[23]

Where does Jesus fit in?

The New Testament never names Jesus as a card-carrying member of any of these four groups. While it seems clear that Jesus identified least of all with the Sadducees, we do see

---

22 Of the four Gospels, Luke is the only one who tells us that Jesus and John were relatives. Luke only says that Jesus' mother, Mary, and John's mother, Elizabeth, knew each other and visited together prior to the birth of their sons (and the child, John, leaps in Elizabeth's womb). Not even Luke, though, tells us of a time when Jesus and John acknowledge their blood-relation. We are left to speculate as to whether they spent time together as children or young adults.

23 To learn more, we recommend *The Dead Sea Scrolls Today* by James C. VanderKam (Eerdmans 2010).

some similarities between Jesus and the other three sects (Pharisees, Essenes, and Zealots).

Jesus in his context

During his ministry, Jesus was sometimes called rabbi which was a way that Pharisees were often addressed. Like the Pharisees, Jesus also interpreted the law and showed a great love for it. We see this in his opening words in the Sermon on the Mount:

> ***Do not think that I have come to abolish the Law or the Prophets; I have not come to abolish them but to fulfill them.***
>
> **Matthew 5:17**

The word "fulfill" can also be translated "complete." Jesus and the Pharisees shared a concern for the living out of the commandments of God.[24]

Like the Essenes, Jesus withdrew on occasion to the desert, and parts of Jesus' message about the Kingdom of God are similar to John the Baptist's preaching. As we noted above, John seems to have a lot in common with the Essenes.

Though Jesus would have rejected the Zealots' use of violence against Rome, he was nevertheless zealous for the law and the temple. In fact, according to one Gospel writer, as Jesus was driving the merchants out of the temple, his disciples were reminded of Psalm 69:9, "...Zeal for your house will consume me" (John 2:17).

For too long Christians have tried to extract Jesus from Judaism. But when we do this, we miss out on so much. We

24 In the decades after the death and resurrection of Jesus, Rabbinic Judaism looked back and claimed to be the heir of the Pharisees. The Rabbinic movement began after the destruction of the temple in 70 A.D., and the rabbis arose as leaders in place of priests.

will learn more about Jesus by understanding him as a part of his own context rather than attempting to insulate him from it. This Christmas, may we learn to receive Jesus' Jewishness as the wonderful gift that it is.

CHAPTER FIVE

John the Baptist: Preparing for Christmas

Preparing for Christmas can be all-consuming. It takes a lot of time, money, and energy to cross everything off of your to-do list. There are cards to send and decorations to hang. Our calendars fill up with parties and special programs at school or church. We cook and eat an abundance of good food. And, of course, there's shopping.

Getting ready for the Christmas holiday

During their first year of marriage, Wil's wife, Rebecca, had to work every day of the Thanksgiving holiday. This meant they could not travel home to be with family that year. Rebecca's work schedule also prevented her from shopping on Black Friday (the day after Thanksgiving when the insanity of the Christmas shopping season starts). At her request, Wil agreed to venture out to the mall by himself to buy gifts for members of the family. No big deal, he thought.

That morning, Wil took his time getting up and out the door. He didn't bother to make a list, and he had no plan about which stores to go to first. He would just go with the list in his head and see what appealed to him when he got to the mall.

Upon arrival, it looked as if the whole city was already at

the mall. It took a long time to find a parking spot. The aisles of the stores were so congested that Wil could hardly examine any of the merchandise. He spent several hours shopping but came home empty-handed. Lack of preparation doomed Wil's Black Friday shopping trip before it ever began. It's been almost twenty years since that dreadful day, and Wil has still not mustered the courage to enter a retail establishment on Black Friday again. Although, you will be glad to know he has learned to take full advantage of Cyber Monday instead.

Preparing for Christ at Christmas: Advent and John the Baptist

The churches that we pastor follow the Christian Liturgical Calendar (or Church Year). Churches that follow this calendar celebrate Advent as the season leading up to Christmas. Advent is comprised of the four Sundays before December 25. It is a time of prayer and devotion. Part of the collective wisdom of the Church Year teaches us that we are not ready for Christmas.

We don't want to get to Bethlehem too quickly. We may desire to focus more on Jesus this Christmas. Without a plan, though, we won't fare any better than Wil did on his Black Friday shopping trip. Advent is a plan of preparation for Christmas. Thankfully, we are not the ones who do the preparing. In Advent, God is preparing us for the gift of Jesus.

One of the biblical characters we spend time with during Advent is John the Baptist. John was a fiery preacher whose sermons drew people out of the cities and into the desert to hear him and receive baptism. If he appeared on the scene today, he would be a street preacher.

The story of John begins in the first chapter of Luke when an angel appears to John's father, Zechariah, in the temple to tell him that he and his wife, Elizabeth, will have a son.

...Do not be afraid, Zechariah; your prayer has been heard. Your wife Elizabeth will bear you a son, and you are to call him John. He will be a joy and delight to you, and many will rejoice because of his birth, for he will be great in the sight of the Lord. He is never to take wine or other fermented drink, and he will be filled with the Holy Spirit even before he is born. He will bring back many of the people of Israel to the Lord their God. And he will go on before the Lord, in the spirit and power of Elijah, to turn the hearts of the parents to their children and the disobedient to the wisdom of the righteous—to make ready a people prepared for the Lord.

Luke 1:13-17

As an adult, John's message was simple: repent of your sins. Turn from your wicked ways. Be on the lookout for the one who is coming. The one whose arrival John spoke of was Jesus.

John began this prophetic message even before his birth. His impending arrival prompted his father, Zechariah, to repent for his failure to believe the promise of the angel. While still inside Elizabeth's womb, John alerted his mother, possibly by means of a swift kick to the ribs, to the presence of Christ in Mary's womb. Elizabeth's joyous response provides Mary encouragement and helps Mary begin to understand the nature of the great work God will do through her child.

When John preached, he never sugarcoated his words.

...You brood of vipers! Who warned you to flee from the coming wrath? Produce fruit in keeping with repentance. And do not begin to say to yourselves, 'We have Abraham as our father.' For I tell you that out of these stones God can raise up children for Abraham. The ax is already at the root of the trees, and every tree that does not produce good fruit will be cut down and thrown into the fire.

Luke 3:7-9

If that sounds a bit unseasonal, more like Scrooge than Tiny Tim, it gets worse. John goes on to say of Jesus:

> ***I baptize you with water...but He [Jesus] will baptize you with the Holy Spirit and fire. His winnowing fork is in his hand, and, he will clear his threshing floor, gathering his wheat into the barn and burning up the chaff with unquenchable fire.***
>
> **Matthew 3:11-12**

That's not the sort of thing that makes you want to sing, "It's the Most Wonderful Time of the Year." John the Baptist isn't very Christmassy. And this is why we need him to help prepare us for Christmas.

An adult Jesus at Christmas

If you've read the Gospels, then you know that John the Baptist shows up to make way, not for baby Jesus, but for Jesus the adult. Luke's Gospel tells us that Jesus was about thirty years old when he started calling his first disciples.[25] So why do we talk about John preparing us for Christmas? Isn't Christmas about Jesus' arrival on earth as a baby?

Yes, it is. However, Christmas is originally a celebration of the doctrine of the Incarnation (God becoming human in the flesh of Jesus Christ).[26] Christmas celebrates Jesus' birth, but it does more than that. At Christmas, we give thanks for all that Jesus is for us.

On your birthday, a loved one might get out some of your baby pictures. This could be to say either, "I remember, not so long ago, when you were just entering the world" or "Wow! This

25 Luke 3:23

26 See chapter 1 for more on the Incarnation.

was a long time ago. You're getting old!" But on a birthday we don't just focus on what someone was like as a baby. We celebrate the person that they are, all that they mean to us.

The same is true for the festival of Jesus' birth. Christmas is about Jesus' birth, life, death, resurrection, ascension, and ongoing presence with us through the Holy Spirit. During Advent, John the Baptist calls us to repent as a way of preparing to receive the fullness of the gift of Jesus.

What is repentance?

Matthew, Mark, and Luke each tell us that the heart of John the Baptist's ministry was calling people to repent of their sins.[27] Repentance is one of those churchy words that we use all the time, but we may be less clear on what it means than we care to admit. For some Christians, to repent means to feel sorrow or to apologize.

When Paul was a child, he would occasionally get into fights with his younger brother (ok, maybe more than occasionally). These scuffles would usually end with his brother running to their parents in tears. Mom or dad would come to Paul and say, "Apologize to your brother." Paul would mumble, "Sorry..." Then his parents would say, "No, tell him you're sorry. And mean it!" Repentance is often understood like this: telling God you're sorry and really meaning it.

While it's true that remorse is an important part of repentance, there's more to it than that. We should learn, as the hymn says, to mourn our sins. But it's possible to apologize,

27 The Gospel of John (the Fourth Gospel) portrays John the Baptist differently. In the Fourth Gospel, John the Baptist's main purpose is to point people to Jesus. Twice in John, (1:29 & 1:36) John the Baptist sees Jesus and exclaims, "Look, the Lamb of God." Jesus' earliest disciples appear to have been first following John the Baptist, until he tells them to go and start following Jesus (John 1:37-38). Some scholars have suggested that Jesus himself may have originally been a follower of John the Baptist before launching out on his own ministry.

even to feel very badly about having done something wrong, only to repeat the same offense a day or two later. Not only is it possible, it's a predictable pattern for many of us. An apology without a change in behavior is hollow, no matter how sincere or tearful.

When the Old Testament prophets call on God's people to repent, they mean for them to be sorry for their sins and also to return to God. To sin is to stray from God and God's ways. To repent, in the Old Testament, is to turn around and come back home to God.

The New Testament uses the Greek *metanoia* for repentance, a word which carries with it the idea of changing one's mind. Both of these are crucial for receiving God's gift of Jesus. Repentance means transformation, not just a change in the decorations or a rearrangement of the furniture. Jesus comes to bring us back to God and to change our collective and individual mind. The Apostle Paul surely meant something like this when he wrote:

> ***Therefore, I urge you, brothers and sisters, in view of God's mercy...not to conform to the pattern of this world, but be transformed by the renewing of your mind.***
>
> **Romans 12:1-2[28]**

The prophet Isaiah says that all of us are like sheep. We have wandered away from God, following our own self-destructive path (Isaiah 53:6). Isaiah speaks for each of us as individuals and for all humanity. So, the message of repentance is hard news, but it's good news. We are lost. But God has found us.

28 The Greek here provides a nuance that is missing in most English translations. As he often does, the Apostle Paul writes in the indicative rather than the imperative. So, verses like these from Romans literally read "not conforming...being transformed" instead of "don't conform...be transformed." It's subtle but powerful. The Apostle is describing what the transformed life looks like more than he's commanding his readers to do something.

God is calling the whole human family back home.

Repentance and the kingdom

Repentance, for John the Baptist, was about something called "the Kingdom of Heaven." When John started preaching, his first sermon was short:

> ***...Repent for the kingdom of heaven has come near.***
>
> **Matthew 3:2**

The term "Kingdom of Heaven," as we find it in the Gospel of Matthew, is often misinterpreted. Both John and Jesus talk about it, and several of Jesus' most famous parables are about the Kingdom of Heaven.[29] For example,

> ***He [Jesus] told them another parable: 'The kingdom of heaven is like a mustard seed, which a man took and planted in his field. Though it is the smallest of the seeds, yet when it grows, it is the largest of the garden plants and becomes a tree so that the birds of the air come and perch in its branches.'***
>
> **Matthew 13:31-32**

When we hear "the Kingdom of Heaven" we sometimes think that Jesus is talking about the afterlife, the place where we will go when we die. This is understandable, but if we look closely at how both John the Baptist and Jesus speak of this kingdom, we will see that they're describing a present, earthly reality, not just something that awaits us on the other side of death.[30]

---

29 Some of the same teachings and parables are also found, nearly word-for-word, in Mark and Luke. But in those two Gospels the term "Kingdom of God" is used instead of "Kingdom of Heaven." They appear to be slightly different ways of talking about the same thing.

30 As we discussed in chapter 2, the Bible offers us wonderful promises of life beyond death.

A kingdom is a realm where a king rules, a king's territory. At the height of the British Empire, the king of the United Kingdom was the monarch for hundreds of millions of people across the world. Jesus and John the Baptist were born in the kingdom of Augustus Caesar.

When John the Baptist and Jesus talk about "the Kingdom of Heaven," they mean the realm where God reigns and God's will is done. God certainly rules heaven, but God also is the peerless Lord of the earth.

This kingdom is not far off, awaiting us beyond the pearly gates. John the Baptist says that the kingdom is near. This is part of what we are called to change our minds about when we repent. Our mindset has been that God's kingdom is distant. Christians sometimes focus on heaven and streets of gold more than on what God is doing here and now. While eternal life is a big part of the hope we have as Christians, we give up too quickly on hope for life in this world. Have we settled for a Gospel that is inspirational but which makes no real difference in the world?

John the Baptist and Jesus boldly proclaim the presence of the Kingdom of Heaven, God's kingdom, even while Caesar is still on the throne. Repentance is changing our mind about who is really in charge. Christianity is more than a marginally relevant extracurricular activity. When we call Jesus "Lord," we are not saying that he's our personal life coach. Rather, we're making a huge claim: Jesus is Lord of all creation. We repent of reducing Jesus to our advisor instead of our Lord.

The Apostle Paul, for example, proclaims God's victory in Christ over death and the grave (1 Corinthians 15:50-56).

John the Baptist: keeping it weird

Several years ago, we started seeing t-shirts and stickers in Asheville, North Carolina that read, "Keep Asheville Weird." Not long after that the same kind of merchandise began showing up in cities like Louisville, Kentucky and Portland, Oregon. Having spent time in these places, we doubt that this campaign will have difficulty succeeding. Keep Portland weird? Not a problem.

John the Baptist was weird before weird was cool. While the Gospels say almost nothing about Jesus' appearance, Matthew and Mark include details about John's unusual fashion. He wore vintage clothing of camel's hair (a throwback to the prophet Elijah). Also, he ate an organic or paleo diet of locusts and wild honey.

He dressed weird, ate strange things, and preached a harsh message. Yet people left the comfort of Jerusalem to go listen to John in the desert. Most evangelists go where the people are. This one drew the people to himself. Earlier we said that in today's world John would be a street preacher. That's probably right, but instead of preaching on Main Street he would be doing his work on the backroads and in the forgotten parts of town.

This weirdness is what makes John the Baptist the right person to prepare us for Christmas. The usual ways of getting ready for Christmas cause us to miss Jesus each year. We've been preparing for Christmas instead of Jesus. Maybe this year we need to spend a little more time listening closely to John the Baptist and his message of repentance.

Repentance then and now

In seeking to discern what John's message of repentance

might mean for us today, let's ponder how it came across to his first listeners. In the previous chapter, we spoke about four influential communities within first century Judaism: Pharisees, Sadducees, Zealots, and Essenes. Considering how John's message came across to those within each of these communities may help us hear his message afresh for us today.

The **Pharisees** seem to be the group of people within Judaism most committed to living out their faith through their everyday lives, and for this they should be commended. Some within this group eventually become Jesus' disciples, while others draw harsh criticism from Jesus for being more concerned about following the letter of their religious laws than the Spirit of God.

Some of us have, no doubt, often made life about following rules. We subconsciously believe God loves us more when we follow the rules well, so we define ourselves by our performance as a professional, as a parent, as a spouse, as a friend, as an athlete. This way of living leads us to believe God is more pleased with us than with those who don't perform as well as we do, though we would never say so in polite company. When we find ourselves taking on performance-based identities, John's message of repentance may well call us back to recognizing we all sin and fall short. We ought to celebrate and rejoice in Jesus' grace through which we discover ourselves to be loved magnificently, even in our worst moments, and through which we discover others to be loved and valued just as magnificently as we are.

The **Sadducees**, with their lack of belief in the afterlife and focus on acquiring political power, may have been comprised of many pragmatists, not unlike many of us, who had trouble believing all the religious stories they heard and who did not mind to get their hands dirty and make compromises to help society move in the right direction. Among the Sadducees, there were likely a number who saw religion and politics in purely opportunistic terms.

How easy it is for us today to turn our religion and relationships into means for wealth acquisition and power consolidation? There is a reason why Christian churches proclaiming the prosperity gospel - "believe in Jesus and do what we say and you will be successful and wealthy" - are rampant throughout many parts of the world. When we are tempted by the siren calls of wealth and power, John the Baptist's message of repentance may lead us to remember Jesus' words:

> ***"...whoever wants to become great among you must be your servant, and whoever wants to be first must be your slave -- just as the Son of Man did not come to be served, but to serve, and to give his life as a ransom for many."***
>
> **Matthew 20:26-28**

If we take these words seriously, we will be led to repent by rededicating ourselves to a life of service and sacrificial love, all for the sake of loving one another as Jesus loves us, not to receiving any external praise or reward.

The **Zealots** were some of the most passionate, faith-filled people in ancient Israel. They also were often willing to resort to violent and deceptive means to accomplish their ends: assassinations, ambushes, and poisonings were all in their playbook to overthrow their Roman oppressors. History is littered with the aftermath of Christians who thought their religious beliefs gave them the right to violate their own ethical standards to accomplish their purposes. In fact, one of the primary qualms many people have with Christianity is the hypocrisy they observe in the lives of Christians.

We doubt you will have to think very hard to recall a time when you compromised your values to accomplish your goals. Perhaps today, John the Baptist's message of repentance to you means recognizing faithfulness in failure is a greater witness than success without integrity.

How can we not admire the spiritual hunger of the **Essenes**? They were willing to forsake many of the material comforts of life to seek God in the desert. When cultural temptations came their way, they removed themselves so they could not be tempted. Surely, some of the Essenes exhibited the same beautiful depth of spiritual devotion we later observed in the very best of the monastic traditions in Christianity.

Most likely, while some Essenes withdrew from the larger society for the highest of purposes, others withdrew from the world because it was simply easier to live in a self-contained ethnically and religious homogeneous community than to deal with the difficulty and complexity of living in a more diverse community. Have you been guilty of shying away from reaching out to neighbors or co-workers in need because they do not think, look, or act like you? We certainly have. Could it be that repentance for you this Christmas might mean opening your eyes and your heart to their needs?

Repent, let go, prepare

John's message is radical. Repentance means renewal. It's a new start, a revolution in our thinking and living. John asks us (tells us) to let go of our to-do lists, even to repent of them, and let God prepare us for Jesus. John calls us to turn around, come home, and change our mind. We do the same things every year, and for some reason we expect different results. This year, invite John the Baptist to your Christmas party. He'll wreck it. And you'll be glad he did.

CHAPTER SIX

A Virgin Birth? Seriously?

Several years ago, megachurch pastor Andy Stanley made national headlines when he claimed that people can be Christians without believing that Mary was a virgin when she gave birth to Jesus. Stanley noted that many of the first Christians knew little or nothing about the Christmas story. After all, only two of the four Gospels (Matthew and Luke) tell us anything about Jesus' birth. Mark, which is probably the oldest of the Gospels, says nothing about the birth of Jesus. And John's Gospel doesn't include any stories about Jesus' birth in Bethlehem, either.

Could it be that these two writers and the Christian communities they came from didn't know anything about the circumstances of Jesus' birth? The first Christians became followers of Jesus through the proclamation of Jesus' lordship and his resurrection from the dead.[31] All of this led Andy Stanley to conclude that the virgin birth is not a deal-breaker. People can follow Jesus without being certain about this particular doctrine.

While Stanley angered a lot of people, he raised an inter-

---

31 Many Church Historians believe that the earliest confessions of faith were "Jesus is Lord" and "Christ is risen."

esting question. How many different doctrines do you have to accept before your faith counts? Where is the line?

Stanley's question leads us to ponder how the story of the virgin birth should shape our beliefs and whether it should shape our beliefs at all. To do so, let's first consider some of the major questions people ask about the virgin birth.

What about basic biology?

Both of us affirm the virgin birth (we don't cross our fingers behind our backs when we say the Apostles' Creed), but we recognize that it is difficult for some people to embrace. Wasn't this biological fact covered in the eighth-grade health class unit on sexual reproduction? Didn't those charts and diagrams settle this once and for all?

Maybe what makes this challenging is not the question of whether or not God could make something like the virgin birth happen. Presumably, if one believes in God, especially the God who raised Jesus from the dead, then at least in theory the possibility of virgin birth can't be ruled out. If there is such a God, then God can do whatever God wants. The better question may be why. Why would God do something like this? One might be able to see why God responded to the crucifixion by raising Jesus from the dead. But why would God choose to sidestep basic biology when Jesus could have been conceived, shall we say, the old-fashioned way?

Is the virgin birth actually biblical?

Christians believe that the Old Testament prophet Isaiah spoke of Jesus' birth hundreds of years before it happened. The Gospel of Matthew makes the link for us between the virgin birth and Isaiah:

All of this took place to fulfill what the Lord had said through the prophet: 'The virgin will be with child and will give birth to a son, and they will call him Immanuel' which means, 'God with us.'

Matthew 1:22-23

But did Isaiah actually speak about a virgin giving birth or was Isaiah only talking about a young woman?

The Old Testament was originally written mostly in Hebrew. Matthew, like the rest of the New Testament, was written in Greek. So, Matthew's quotations from the Old Testament are all in Greek, not Hebrew. The reason for this, most likely, is that Matthew used the Greek translation of the Old Testament called the Septuagint. Matthew's use of the Septuagint may account for the differences and disagreement in understanding what Isaiah's prophecy means.[32]

The Greek word that Matthew uses in his citation of Isaiah 7:14 (following the Septuagint) is *parthenonos*, which is usually translated virgin. But in the Hebrew version of Isaiah, the word is *almah*, which more often means a young woman. In that ancient culture, the default assumption would have been that an almah, a young woman not yet married, would have indeed also been a virgin. However, the Hebrew Old Testament more regularly uses the word *betula* for virgin.

This difference has led many people to ask whether there was ever really an Old Testament prophecy about a virgin birth to

---

32 In 1952, a new translation of the Bible was published called the Revised Standard Version. It created widespread controversy among some Christians for translating the Hebrew word almah in Isaiah 7:14 not as "virgin" but "young woman." Some people went so far as to burn copies of the Revised Standard Version, calling it the devil's Bible, because, they said, it denied the virgin birth. For so many reasons, this was a terrible overreaction. The translators of the Revised Standard Version did not deny the virgin birth at all. The change in translation was in Isaiah. In the New Testament passages in question, the Revised Standard Version still used the word "virgin." And, its rendering of the Christmas stories in Matthew and Luke did nothing to undermine this part of the story of Jesus.

begin with.[33] Perhaps it was just a prophecy concerning a young woman who was going to have a baby. Others have suggested that the early church read this prophecy in Isaiah and then made up the story about Jesus' birth to go along with it.

It may be helpful to think about what it means for prophecy to be fulfilled. The Old Testament prophets did a lot more than simply predict the future. The prophets weren't fortune tellers. Their work addressed their present context, not the distant future. When they did make predictions, it had to do with the immediate consequences of then-current events. In the case of Isaiah 7:14, the prophet's word about the virgin/young woman is a word of comfort to King Ahaz. Isaiah goes on to say that by the time this child, Immanuel, is grown, the two armies that are threatening Ahaz and the people of Judah will be no more. Isaiah probably wouldn't have sought to comfort the king by telling him, "Deliverance from our enemies will come. Just wait seven hundred years."

We should be clear, though, that just because Isaiah was speaking first of all to his own day does not rule out that his prophecies might also speak to the life and ministry of Jesus. Prophecy can be true in more than one setting. There are many other parts of Isaiah that have been read in relation to Jesus. One of the most notable examples is known as the Suffering Servant:

> ***He was despised and rejected by mankind, a man of suffering, and familiar with pain... Surely he took up our pain and bore our suffering ... But he was pierced for our transgressions, he was crushed for our iniquities; the punishment that brought us peace was on him, and by his wounds we are healed.***
>
> **Isaiah 53:3-5**

33 This debate goes back much further than 1952. In the 100's A.D., the early Christian writer Justin Martyr defended the belief in the virgin birth in his dialogues with a Jewish man named Trypho.

These words had meaning in the days when they were first spoken, but for the early church passages like this leapt off the page. They read them and immediately thought of Jesus. While Isaiah could have originally been talking about Israel itself or an individual, whose identity is lost to history, it was obvious to the first Christians that these verses describe Jesus. Thankfully, we don't have to choose one or the other. Prophecy can be both a word from God in its day and time and a word for other times in the life of God's people as well.

Not an original idea?

Jesus is not the only historical figure believed to have been born of a virgin. Stories circulated in the ancient world of the virgin birth of Alexander the Great, Caesar Augustus, and other Roman Emperors. Is it possible that Matthew and Luke knew of these narratives and decided to apply them to the life of Jesus? Other religious traditions, such as Buddhism and Islam, also have stories like this about the founders of their faiths.

This has led some to suggest that the Gospel accounts of the virgin birth are simply an ancient literary device for signifying the greatness of a hero. Perhaps Matthew and Luke added their stories about Jesus' birth to show that, even though he was a Jewish peasant, he was as powerful as Caesar or any other great earthly ruler.

One way we could respond would be to say, "Well, all of the other stories about virgin births are lies, and ours is true." While, at the end of the day, we do believe our Lord was born of a virgin and we doubt (even disbelieve) the claims about other historical figures, responding in this way strikes us as defensive and reactionary.

It is tempting for us to respond similarly when confronted

with the reality of other religious traditions: they are wrong, we are right, end of story. Again, this response seems rooted in fear. It's a kind of fear that puts on blinders and pretends that other religions don't even exist.

We can also acknowledge the existence of other faith traditions and other stories of virgin births without becoming relativists. It is possible to treat people of other religions with deep respect without adopting the idea that we all really believe the same things but just express it differently, or that it doesn't matter what you believe as long as you're sincere.

We believe God chose to take on flesh through a virgin birth – a circumstance humans already regarded as a symbol of a great destiny – as a way of making known to the world the source of all true greatness and power.

What does the Bible say?

Now that we've surveyed some of the questions and objections people have, we should ask what the Bible actually says about the virgin birth.

What do the Gospels say?

Matthew and Luke are the only two writers in the New Testament that talk about the virgin birth. Yet, they do so very differently.[34] So let's look at how they each tell this part of the story of Jesus' birth.

Matthew

As we pointed out in chapter 3, Matthew's genealogy ends surprisingly. Matthew does not call Joseph the father of

34 Most scholars agree that Matthew and Luke worked independently of each other. It appears that they didn't collaborate and one did not copy the other (while this is the overwhelming schol-

Jesus. Instead, he says that Joseph is the husband of Mary who is the mother of Jesus. She is the only one explicitly named as a parent of Jesus in the genealogy. Then Matthew moves into the story of Jesus' birth:

> ***This is how the birth of Jesus Christ came about: His mother Mary was pledged to be married to Joseph, but before they came together, she was found to be pregnant through the Holy Spirit.***
>
> **Matthew 1:18**

Imagine that you don't know where the story is headed. You wouldn't necessarily know what is meant by the statement that Mary is pregnant through the Holy Spirit. Joseph certainly doesn't know at this point. He apparently believes that Mary has become pregnant by another man, and he chooses to divorce her quietly.

Then the angel helps Joseph and the readers begin to grasp what is going on here. The angel visits Joseph in a dream and says to him:

> ***Joseph son of David, do not be afraid to take Mary home as your wife, because what is conceived in her is from the Holy Spirit.***
>
> **Matthew 1:20**

Yet, there is still room for confusion. Just because the Holy Spirit is involved doesn't mean that a human father isn't in the picture. The angel could mean that in spite of appearances, and a less than desirable situation, the Holy Spirit is at work in this unexpected pregnancy. It's the narrator, Matthew, who makes it plain by telling us that this fulfills Isaiah 7:14:

---

arly consensus, there are some exceptions). If this is true, then we're not talking about a case of either Matthew or Luke inventing the story of the virgin birth. Rather, the tradition of Mary's virginity was something they each knew and wrote about in their own unique way.

The virgin will conceive and give birth to a son....[35]

Matthew 1:23

This is the one and only use of the word "virgin" in Matthew's Christmas story (Matthew doesn't use the word again until chapter 25 in Jesus' parable of the ten virgins). It's also the first and last reference to the virgin birth in Matthew's entire Gospel.

Joseph seems to understand what the angel means. He does what he's told to do. He calls off the divorce, marries Mary, and adopts her child as his own. And the circumstances of Mary's pregnancy are never discussed again in Matthew.

Luke

Luke uses the word "virgin" two times in his Christmas story, both in the introduction of Mary[36]:

In the sixth month of Elizabeth's pregnancy, God sent the angel Gabriel to Nazareth, a town in Galilee, to a virgin pledged to be married to a man named Joseph, a descendant of David. The virgin's name was Mary.

Luke 1:26-27

The reader knows of Mary's virginity from the beginning of the story. Luke leaves no room for a question of whether

35 Matthew is most likely quoting the Greek Septuagint (what we know as the Old Testament; there was no New Testament yet), which probably would have been the version of the Scriptures that he knew best. This is as opposed to the Hebrew text of the Old Testament, which Matthew may not have had access to at all. And the Greek word used in the Septuagint is parthenos, which is correctly translated as virgin.

36 Some translations (such as the NIV) also use the word in Luke 1:34 where Mary responds to the angel's announcement that she will have a son: "How can this be since I am a virgin?" But the Greek text says literally not, "...since I am a virgin" but "...since I do not know a man."

another man (any man) might be Jesus' biological father. Whereas the drama in Matthew's account of the virgin birth centers on Joseph's acceptance of Mary and her Holy Spirit-conceived son, Luke's drama is found in celebrating the God who does the impossible.

The theme of impossibility is first sounded in the opening verses of Luke when the angel Gabriel tells a priest named Zechariah that he and his wife Elizabeth will be parents. Zechariah doesn't believe it. He and Elizabeth have never been able to have children, because, Luke tells us, Elizabeth was barren. Besides that, they were too old anyway. But, like another biblical couple, Abraham and Sarah in Genesis, Zechariah and Elizabeth become first-time parents in their old age.

When Gabriel tells Mary that she will have a son, not just any son but Jesus, who will reign over God's people like David, she understandably asks how this is possible. And Gabriel delights in telling Mary,

> ***The Holy Spirit will come on you, and the power of the Most High will overshadow you. So the holy one to be born will be called the Son of God. Even Elizabeth your relative is going to have a child her old age, and she who was said to be unable to conceive is in her sixth month. For no word from God will ever fail.***
>
> **Luke 1:35-37**

After Gabriel leaves, Mary goes to visit Elizabeth and the two of them celebrate the impossible things that God is doing and will do.

Unlike Matthew, Luke says nothing about how Joseph received this news. In fact, in the scene after Mary's visit to Elizabeth, Luke implies that their engagement moved forward without any difficulty.

Like Matthew, Luke never mentions the virgin birth again in his Gospel. The closest that Luke comes is in the opening lines of his genealogy:

> ***Now Jesus himself was about thirty years old when he began his ministry. He was the son, so it was thought, of Joseph....***
>
> **Luke 3:23**

It is surprising, to say the least, that in both Matthew and Luke nothing else is ever said by the narrators or any other characters about Jesus' miraculous birth.

What does the Apostle Paul say about Jesus' birth?

Not much. Paul (sort of) mentions Jesus' birth a couple of times. But he says nothing about the details of the birth. No word about Bethlehem, Joseph, or Mary.

The two best-known references to Jesus' birth in Paul's letters are in Romans and Galatians.[37]

> ***Paul, a servant of Christ Jesus, called to be an apostle and set apart for the gospel of God - the gospel he promised beforehand through his prophets in the Holy Scriptures regarding his Son, who as to his earthly life was a descendant of David....***
>
> **Romans 1:1-3**

> ***But when the time had fully come, God sent his Son, born of a woman, born under the law, to redeem those under the law....***
>
> **Galatians 4:4**

The passage from Romans is really less about Jesus' birth than it is his Davidic ancestry. And the verse from Galatians

---

37 Some translations render Philippians 2:7b as "...being born in human likeness...." This is a possible translation of the Greek (ginomai), but it is also often translated "to become" or "to happen."

says nothing about the details of Jesus' birth. Paul simply states that Jesus was born. This would have been a good place to mention Mary or even the virgin birth.

Toward the close of 1 Corinthians, Paul reminds his readers of the core teachings of the faith that he shared with them when he founded the church in Corinth. Scholars have long noted that these verses look a lot like an early form of the Apostles Creed:

> ***...I want to remind you of the gospel I preached to you...for what I received I passed on to you as of first importance:***
>
> > ***that Christ died for our sins according to the Scriptures,***
> > ***that he was buried,***
> >
> > ***that he was raised on the third day according to the Scriptures,***
> > ***and that he appeared to [Peter] and then to the Twelve....***
>
> **1 Corinthians 15:1,3-5**

For the Apostle these are the essentials: Jesus died, was buried, was raised, and appeared. What's missing? Any word about Jesus being born to a virgin named Mary.

On the one hand, it's not shocking that the Apostle Paul says almost nothing about Jesus' birth. He has very little to say in general about Jesus' life and teaching. Most of the Apostle's proclamation of Christ is about his death and resurrection. One of the very few places where Paul actually quotes Jesus directly is found in 1 Corinthians 11:23-25, where he talks about the tradition of the Lord's Supper.

On the other hand, this omission does raise some interesting questions. Did Paul know anything about the virgin birth? If so, then why doesn't he ever talk about it, celebrate it, or defend it? If he did not know of it, then why? Was it not shared with him as one of the central elements of the faith? We could, of course, ask the same questions of things like healing stories, the Lord's Prayer, and the parables, none of which are mentioned by the Apostle in his letters.

Paul preached and wrote before the Gospels were written.[38] The church was in its earliest stages, and the news that was rocking the world was the message of a crucified and risen God. It sounds strange to say, but the early church was so consumed with this earth-shattering news that it hadn't yet taken time to reflect on other parts of Jesus' life and teaching.

The other major thing that consumed Pauline Christianity (the church in Paul's day) was the question of how the Gentiles would be welcomed into this movement. Between preaching the cross and addressing the urgent matter of gentile-inclusion, Paul's pastoral plate was full.

So, it's not fair to say that because Paul doesn't mention it, the virgin birth is obviously not historical. Nor is it fair to say that because other matters were so much more important (e.g. the cross and resurrection) that the virgin birth is unimportant. The most we can say is that the virgin birth was, along with a lot of other things about Jesus, overshadowed by the message about the cross and resurrection.

Is the story of the virgin birth a cover-up?

This may seem like a strange question, but it's one that has persisted across the centuries. Sometimes it's speculation, and other times it's accusation.

Did Mary have an affair with a Roman soldier, as one early critic of Christianity claimed, or was she a prostitute who

38 Or at least before the Gospels were completed.

became pregnant, as other opponents of the faith suggested? Did the first Christians devise the story of the virgin birth to hide Jesus' shameful origins?

The earliest record of this kind of accusation comes from the late second century A.D. It became a common charge among those who opposed the spread of the Christian faith. John 8:41 has sometimes been cited as evidence of this conspiracy. Here Jesus is in the middle of a back-and-forth with of his critics, some of whom, John says, used to believe in him. As the exchange heats up, so does the rhetoric, and these detractors say to Jesus:

> ***... 'We are not illegitimate children,' they protested. 'The only Father we have is God himself.'***
>
> **John 8:41**

Some people have suggested that Jesus' opponents knew of rumors that Mary had given birth to him out of wedlock. If so, then perhaps what his antagonists mean is,

"We aren't illegitimate (like you)!"

Accusations and innuendos like this could have been used to try to discredit Jesus. This is clearly what Jesus detractors are doing a few verses later in the same chapter:

> ***...Aren't we right in saying that you are a Samaritan and demon-possessed?***
>
> **John 8:48**

Why would they call him a Samaritan? Because Jews and Samaritans did not get along, and it probably would have been an insult to a Jewish person to be called a Samaritan.

But there's more than that. In the John 4:1-30, Jesus spends time talking with a Samaritan woman beside a well, and as a result of their conversation, John's Gospel tells us, many Samaritans came to believe in Jesus. So Jesus' opponents could be trying to call attention to his scandalous association with and sympathy for Samaritans.

The charge of demon possession is otherwise not mentioned in John's Gospel, but it does come up in the Gospel of Mark:

> ***And the teachers of the law who came down from Jerusalem said, 'He is possessed by Beelzebub! By the prince of demons he is driving out demons.'***
>
> **Mark 3:22**

Jesus' opponents likely did not make up the charges that he was a Samaritan and demon-possessed on the spot. Instead, they appear to be alluding to gossip that was already swirling around Jesus. Could the Gospel stories of Jesus' birth have been concocted to refute accusations such as these?

These are interesting questions, and we don't want to be too quick to dismiss them. However, it seems to us, following several leading scholars, that the accusations of Jesus' illegitimacy developed mostly after the Gospels were written. This means that it's highly unlikely that the belief in the virgin birth would have been a cover-up-like response, trying to hide the true story of Jesus' parents. Rather, it's the conspiracy theories themselves that are the response to the Gospel accounts of the virgin birth.

Had Matthew and Luke been worried, knowing about such rumors as they wrote, then surely they would have included something like Matthew's word about the report of the guards after Jesus' resurrection:

> ***When the chief priests had met with the elders and devised a plan, they gave the soldiers a large sum of money, telling them, 'You are to say, His disciples came during the night and stole him away while we were asleep'.... So the soldiers took the money and did as they were instructed. And this story has been widely circulated among the Jews to this very day.***
>
> **Matthew 28:12-13, 15**

If anything, it's striking at how unconcerned Matthew and Luke are about how this story will be received. If there are any rumors in the air at the time of their writing, neither author addresses them.

What the virgin birth of Jesus does NOT mean

Paul (the co-author of this book, not the Apostle) can remember a high school youth retreat when a well-meaning leader fumbled through a lesson on the virgin birth. The basic point was this: Jesus was born of a virgin so that he would not be the product of a sexual union that involved sin and lust. Similarly, Wil recalls a Sunday school teacher saying that the virgin birth made Jesus pure and free from sin. These sorts of statements represent a common misconception (sorry for the pun) about the virgin birth.

Matthew and Luke had many reasons for telling us of the virgin birth. Disdain for sex was surely not among their reasons.

But, if we're honest, we can acknowledge that the church doesn't have the greatest history when it comes to conversations about sex. Our sex-talk has often been dominated by fear. Unfortunately, because Christians are afraid of the power of sexual desire, and especially of the thought of our children negotiating those desires, we sometimes misread the Bible in light of our fears.

The reasons for the church's complicated relationship with sex are beyond the scope of this book. While we don't have time here to go into the history of the church's theology (or lack of theology) of sex, we do want to point out that a fearful approach is not biblical.

Too often we Christians have projected our fears onto the Bible. Yet, the Bible celebrates sex as one of God's great gifts. It's true that both the Old and New Testament acknowledge the potential for this wonderful gift, like any other gift, to be abused and become destructive. But the Bible is not fearful of sex.

This is important for Christians and for skeptics. Skeptics are often quick to dismiss the Bible and Christianity as prudish or anti-sex. Admittedly, Christians have given skeptics plenty of reasons to see us this way. Still, Christianity also has many writers and thinkers who have reflected beautifully on the topic of sex. We have noticed that many skeptics tend to judge Christians based on the loudest (and sometimes most inarticulate) spokespersons. This judgment based on generalization is an all too human habit that both Christians and non-Christians alike occasionally fall into.

What does it mean?

Let's think back to Andy Stanley's assertion that someone can be a Christian without believing in the virgin birth. Broadly speaking, he may be right. And certainly, if you're struggling to wrap your heart and mind around the doctrine of the virgin birth, that's okay. Yet, as pastors, we would never advise someone to give up on the virgin birth. Keep struggling.

The problem with the way that Stanley deemphasizes the virgin birth is that for two thousand years Christians have believed that this part of the story tells us something crucial about who Jesus is. Historically, the church has not treated the virgin birth as an add-on or optional. We don't want to be too heavy-handed here, but it's worth asking what the virgin birth teaches us about the work of God in Jesus. How is our understanding of Jesus enriched by this element of his story?

God's creative, life-giving power

Many theologians have pointed to the parallel between the virgin birth and God's creation of the cosmos in Genesis. God creates everything out of nothing. God did not require raw material that someone else had prepared. All life has its beginning in God. The virgin birth witnesses to this awesome power of God to give life. God is completely free to bring life in whatever way God wants.

Across the millennia, preachers have also proclaimed that the virgin birth foreshadows the resurrection. Both represent biological impossibilities. Virgins don't give birth. Dead bodies don't breathe again. Yet, the God whose Holy Spirit overshadowed Mary, breathed life once again into the dead body of Jesus. In the words of the angel Gabriel, 'nothing is impossible with God.'

The Son of God from the beginning

The virgin birth is one way of expressing that Jesus is the Son of God from the very beginning. From our earliest days, Christians have affirmed that Jesus is both fully human and fully divine.

This historic affirmation is different from saying that Jesus is half-human and half-divine. Such a "half-and-half" doctrine goes back at least as far as a bishop in the fifth century A.D. named Nestorius (the church officially rejected his teachings on the nature of Jesus).

Nor do Christians believe that Jesus is a blend or hybrid of God and humanity. In this case, Jesus would not be truly human. He would be something like God in the shell of a human. This idea of a blended Jesus is associated with, among others, a bishop from the fourth century A.D. named Apollinarius (the church also rejected his teaching on the nature of Jesus).

Another understanding of Jesus that Christians have ruled out along the way is called *adoptionism*. This is the belief that Jesus was not born as the Son of God but was adopted, chosen to be the messiah at some point prior to his ministry. Those who subscribe to this teaching usually identify Jesus' baptism as the point at which he was adopted as God's Son. When Jesus emerges from the water, he sees the heavens torn open and God's voice says,

> ***...You are my Son, whom I love; with you I am well pleased.***
>
> **Mark 1:11**

Adoptionism is often appealing to people who have difficulty affirming that Jesus is God. With adoptionism, Jesus is not necessarily divine. He is seen as a great human or at least a human being who was chosen to do great things for God. Christians have historically rejected adoptionism.

A woman at the center of the story

Mary becomes the mother of Jesus, the God-bearer, unaided by any man. As we've already noted, Matthew's way of putting Mary, rather than Joseph, at the climax of the genealogy that opens his Gospel is astonishing. Additionally, Luke focuses the birth story almost solely on Mary. Joseph is mentioned in Luke, but he never speaks, and only a mere handful of action verbs are associated with him.[39] God does not ask Joseph's permission. God works directly through Mary, unmediated by her husband.

How tragic that for nearly two thousand years Christians have seemed to think that only men can be leaders in the church. Mary is the first minister of the Gospel, the one who is called by God to bring us Jesus Christ. Mary shows us all, men and women, what Christian discipleship looks like.

The wonderful why

As we move toward the close of this discussion, we return to a question that's more meaningful than, "Did it happen?" The question of historicity is important. But the essential question is "why."

Let's say that you believe that it happened, that Jesus really was born of the Virgin Mary. Great. It probably didn't take you very long to make up your mind on that one. And once you've decided, it's more or less settled.

The question that will take a lifetime to try to answer, though, is why. Why did God choose to send Jesus this way? We will never be able to answer it fully, because you can always go deeper. Only God finally knows.

Do you have to believe in the virgin birth in order to be a Christian? Maybe that's the wrong way to look at it. It's not so much that we have to believe it. It's that we get to believe it. Believing in Jesus is a gift. We are invited to believe that

39 We will have more to say on these themes in our upcoming chapter on Mary and Joseph.

he was born of the Virgin Mary, crucified for our sins, raised on the third day, ascended, is sitting in power at the Father's right hand, and is coming again in glory.

The virgin birth shows us when God chose to become human, God did not become mostly human and a little divine. Nor did God choose to appear in the fullness of divinity with a few human characteristics added on in order to be more accessible. In Jesus, we see the very fullness of God and true essence of what it means to be human. Fully human and fully God, able to relate to our weaknesses while showing us the eternal nature of God. What a gift!

CHAPTER SEVEN

Mary and Joseph: The First Disciples

Every December we are flooded with commercials for expensive gifts, especially cars. One memorable ad that recurs each year is by Lexus: a man unwraps a very small box and inside it is a key...to his brand-new Lexus! It's parked on his lawn with a huge red bow on the hood. His wife and family all come outside to watch him play with his new toy. As the camera pulls back you can also see what a nice house they live in.

These commercials apparently appeal to some people. It's not anyone that we know, but more than a few people must be surprising their spouse with a luxury car for Christmas. Otherwise, why would they keep producing new versions of these ads year after year?

When most of us, however, see things like this, we are not persuaded to splurge on an expensive car for Christmas. We cannot relate very well to the people in these commercials. Even by American standards the families depicted here are quite affluent. And compared with the majority of the world's population, anyone who can afford a $60,000 car is far richer than most of the people on earth.

The real Christmas story, by contrast, gives us Mary and

Joseph, who were not people of great wealth. In fact, one of the most extraordinary things about them is how ordinary they appear. Matthew and Luke mention several ancient celebrities and power players in their opening chapters, people like Augustus, Herod, and Quirinius. Mary and Joseph stand out for their utter lack of celebrity. Before they were known for being the parents of Jesus, no one had ever heard of them.

At Christmas it's helpful to remember the anonymity of Mary and Joseph, because we live in a culture that worships celebrities. Just think about how excited people get if they happen to run into someone famous while out in public. Idolizing celebrities leads us to place an inordinately high value on fame. What do we want to be when we grow up? Famous and rich. What are we afraid of being called? Normal and plain.

This celebrity worship is surprisingly rampant in the church and among pastors. Churches end up understanding faithfulness to the Gospel in terms of wealth and certain definitions of success. Congregations are judged as significant based on their size and the number of influential people in their pews. Pastors feel like they are not successful if they aren't serving at a large church. We take so much pride in having the mayor or the millionaire in our church that we overlook Mary and Joseph when they come forward for Communion with their hands open to receive the bread of life.

When Jesus became an adult, he didn't call city council members and professors (or eloquent clergy) to be his first disciples. He went down to the shore and called uncredentialed fishermen. The only person Jesus called who seems to have been anywhere close to power was a tax collector named Matthew.[40] However, a tax collector was anything but

40 Or Levi according to Mark 2:13-14 and Luke 5:27-28.

a celebrity in Roman-occupied Palestine. Christmas is a time to remember that God has different priorities than we do.

Joseph: silently obedient

In the Gospels, Joseph's name is used seven times in Matthew, five times in Luke, twice in John, and not at all in Mark.[41] Even though he's mentioned by name fourteen times, Joseph never speaks. By the time Jesus is grown, Joseph has faded from the picture, while Mary remains throughout Jesus' ministry and is present with the disciples after Jesus' resurrection.[42] Outside the Gospels Joseph is not mentioned in the New Testament, not by the Apostle Paul or even in the book of Acts.

The Gospel of Matthew focuses far more on Joseph than Luke's Gospel does. Even though he's silent, Joseph is at the center of the action in Matthew's first two chapters. Joseph is the one to whom God, through the angel, reveals the miraculous nature and purpose of Mary's pregnancy.[43] Joseph is the one who names Jesus, and Joseph is the one through whom God will continue to guide the holy family by sending angelic messages in dreams. Joseph flees to Egypt to escape the brutal King Herod, leaves Egypt, and settles in a new place, all in response to God's nocturnal guidance. Each time God's messenger visits Joseph's dream, Joseph responds obediently.

The angel never asks Joseph to do something small. Instead, it's one upheaval after another: Proceed with this

41 In Mark 6:3 a hostile home crowd responds to Jesus by asking, "Isn't this the carpenter's son?" They are obviously speaking of Joseph, but they do not use his name.

42 Acts 1:14.

43 Matthew does not tell us whether Mary knew that the child was from the Holy Spirit. When reading Matthew's Gospel on its own terms (meaning that for a moment we pretend that we have only Matthew's account), it looks as though the news is given only to Joseph, who then will inform Mary about the angel's message.

marriage in the face of scandal and uncertainty. Relocate your family to Egypt. Make a new home in Galilee, far from your hometown of Bethlehem. Raise this child as your own. Embrace God's total interruption of your life.

In Luke, not only is Joseph silent, he only has one action verb associated with him.[44] Caesar Augustus has just called for a census of the Roman Empire and then we read:

> ***So Joseph also went up from the town of Nazareth in Galilee to Judea, to Bethlehem the town of David....***
>
> **Luke 2:4**

What does Joseph "do" in Luke? He travels to Bethlehem where Jesus will be born. He says nothing. No speeches, no dialogue, no scenes from his carpenter's shop. During his brief appearance on Luke's stage he stands mostly in the background.

But we see that he is a faithful man. He makes two trips with Jesus to the temple, the first when Jesus is only a few days old and the second for Passover when he is twelve. We can safely assume that he did his best to be a godly father to Jesus.

Why does Joseph disappear from the story?

Most scholars believe that Joseph was older than Mary, maybe a lot older.[45] If they are correct, then perhaps Joseph had died by the time Jesus began his public ministry. With his possible age at the time of their engagement, along with

---

44 While some English translations attribute several action verbs to Joseph in the original Greek text, there is only one action verb attributed directly to Joseph alone.

45 This is an educated guess based on what we know of marriage customs at the time. Nothing in Matthew or Luke tells us specifically how old Joseph and Mary were when Jesus was born.

shorter life expectancy in the ancient world, this is not an unreasonable conclusion. In fact, it's the simplest explanation of his absence from the rest of the story.

Over two thousand years later, countless churches and schools bear the name of St. Joseph. Surely, one reason is to honor a humble, faithful man who sought to follow God's will more than to make a name for himself.

Mary: The first disciple

Matthew and Luke write the most about Mary the mother of Jesus. Mark only uses her name once, and John does not call her by name at all. Instead, John only refers to her as Jesus' mother.[46] She is called once by name in Acts.[47] Like Joseph, Mary's name is not mentioned anywhere by the Apostle Paul or the other writers of the New Testament.

It's the Gospel of Luke that shines the spotlight on Mary. Matthew has her as silent as Joseph. But in Luke we hear Mary speak, follow her travels to see her older relative Elizabeth, and we even get a glimpse of her emotional and spiritual state as the drama unfolds:

> ***But Mary treasured up all these things and pondered them in her heart.***
>
> **Luke 2:19**

It's John who tells us about Mary standing at the foot of the cross. And in Acts, also written by Luke, we see Mary among the disciples who continued to gather together between the time of Jesus' ascension and the descent of the Holy Spirit at Pentecost.

---

46 John 2:1 and John 19:25-27.

47 Acts 1:14.

Certainly, her presence with Jesus during his ministry, at his cross, and with his followers after his resurrection and ascension qualify Mary as a disciple. But Mary is not just *among* the first disciples, she is *the* first disciple. Before she followed the adult Jesus, Mary is the first human being to have her life turned upside down by Jesus. That is the definition of a disciple, someone whose life has been radically altered and completely taken over by Jesus.

Many of us who are Protestants have held Mary at a distance from our faith. We are afraid of doing things that seem too much like Roman Catholicism, and we know something (and probably misunderstand a lot) about Catholic devotion to Mary. So, we let Mary make her weekly appearance in the Apostles Creed, and we bring her out once a year at Christmas. But then she goes back in the box. Consequently, we miss out on so much. Mary is human and not divine, but she shows us that humanity can bear divinity. Put differently, God has created us in such a way that even in our fallenness and frailty we can, with God's help, be God's instruments of grace.

Mary and Joseph interrupted

Both Mary and Joseph, Jesus' first two disciples, give us a model for what it means to welcome Jesus in our lives. Whatever plans they had, individually and together, certainly didn't include anything like this great interruption. To be a disciple means to acknowledge that our lives are not our own. Life can be interrupted by God for God's purposes. We are open to be inconvenienced by God.

Discipleship is hard. We are accustomed to thinking of our lives as our possession. This way of looking at life seems like a given. What should I do with my life? Whatever

I want. Following Jesus, though, makes terms like "my life" problematic.

The two of us grew up in the age before cell phones. It's hard to imagine now, but we actually shared one phone line with the other members of our respective families. In college we shared a phone with our roommates. We can even remember using pay phones on campus (look it up online) and occasionally on the side of the road or in an airport. It's an understatement to say that cell phones have changed everything about how we think of phones. When we were growing up, having caller ID was the rare luxury that not many people had. Now with cell phones we expect to be able to screen every call we receive. In fact, we prefer to screen our calls. Some people let most of their calls go to voicemail (and then never check voicemail), only answering a select few.

For people used to screening our calls, customizing our lives, and limiting interruptions, the stories of Mary and Joseph are incredibly frightening. Life with this God might mean that we, too, will be interrupted by God. The most unsettling thing might be how Mary and Joseph are called to move forward without a roadmap. Even with the angels' visits, the uncertainty is hardly gone. Joseph and Mary must live into this radical new future.

Simeon and Anna

When Mary and Joseph take baby Jesus to the temple, they are met by two unusual characters: an old man named Simeon and a prophet named Anna.[48] Here's how Luke describes Simeon:

48 Some English translations call Anna "prophetess." But the Greek does not read that way. It says "prophet."

Now there was a man in Jerusalem called Simeon, who was righteous and devout. He was waiting for the consolation of Israel, and the Holy Spirit was on him. It had been revealed to him by the Holy Spirit that he would not die before he had seen the Lord's Messiah.

Luke 2:25-26

When Simeon sees Mary and Joseph enter the temple with Jesus, something odd happens. He goes over to them and takes the child out of their arms and starts to sing and pray. What's striking is that Luke says nothing about Mary and Joseph having any idea who Simeon was prior to this moment. He wasn't a priest or any kind of temple official. He was simply a devout man. There would have been lots of devout men there that day. They were in the big city far away from home. This is the Jerusalem temple, not a small country chapel.

Instead of being frightened, Luke says,

The child's father and mother marveled at what was said about him. Then Simeon blessed them....

Luke 2:33-34a

Immediately following Simeon's blessing, the prophet Anna sees them. Anna has remained in the temple worshiping for years. When Anna lays eyes on Jesus, she begins to praise God and then goes and tells everyone about him. As a prophet, Anna is able to discern, just as Simeon did with the guidance of the Holy Spirit, that this is God's Messiah.

As we said in the previous chapter, the church believes that Jesus is fully God and fully human. This staggering claim means a lot of things, one of which is that when we look at Jesus, we see what it means for us to be fully human. In this story we're reminded that to be human is to live in community and entrust our children to the people of God.

Both of us come from strong families and feel like we were raised by excellent parents. Yet our parents alone could not make us who we are today. In bringing us for baptism they handed us over to the church.

When Paul was about seven years old, he was misbehaving at church. One of the other moms began to correct him. Paul looked up at her and said, "You're not my mommy." She said, "That's where you're wrong. Here at church you've got lots of mommies and daddies."

As the story moves forward, Jesus will be raised by Mary and Joseph, but he will also be raised by the much larger community of God's people.

Mary's son lifts up the lowly

Here in the first two chapters of Luke, Jesus is still a baby. When we scan ahead in the narrative, we see some of what Jesus will do.

In his first public message according to Luke, Jesus will lift up the poor and outcast when he speaks the words of Isaiah:

> ***The Spirit of the Lord is on me, because he has anointed me to proclaim good news to the poor. He has sent me to proclaim freedom for the prisoners and recovery of sight for the blind, to set the oppressed free.***
>
> **Luke 4:18**

A little later Jesus will preach another great sermon about God's love for the down and out. This one begins with these words,

> ***...Blessed are you who are poor, for yours is the kingdom of God. Blessed are you who hunger now, for you will be satisfied. Blessed are you who weep now, for you will laugh.***
>
> **Luke 6:20-21**

As Jesus continues his ministry, people on the margins will be drawn to him. He will welcome this, though it will upset some of the religious people:

> ***Now the tax collectors and sinners were all gathering around to hear Jesus. But the Pharisees and the teachers of the law muttered, 'This man welcomes sinners and eats with them.'***
>
> **Luke 15:1-2**

His mother sees all of this in an instant, as she and Elizabeth, who is six months pregnant with John the Baptist at the time, sit there celebrating the surprising grace of God. Mary catches a glimpse of all of these things and more, and she begins to celebrate the work of God, even before it happens, as she sings her song,

> ***My soul glorifies the Lord and my spirit rejoices in God my Savior...he has brought down the rulers from their thrones but has lifted up the humble. He has filled the hungry with good things but has sent the rich away empty.***
>
> **Luke 1:46 & 52-53**

This song has traditionally been called "Mary's Magnificat," from the Latin for her opening words, "My soul magnifies."

Mary and Joseph are two ordinary people who gave themselves to the work of God in the world. In Luke, just before the angel Gabriel visits Mary, we meet another righteous but unexciting couple named Zechariah and Elizabeth. They are older and have no children. Then God shows up and completely changes their lives with the birth of their son, John the Baptist. Dead ends open up to new paths, and there is a way where there was no way.

For Mary and Joseph, as well as Zechariah and Elizabeth, God's unexpected intrusion into their lives leads them to magnify God's love by selflessly responding to the call. Lives of selfless devotion magnify God's love with unmistakable intensity.

Magnifying God's love

Do you remember as a child taking a magnifying glass outside on a sunny summer day and positioning it directly over a dry leaf? It didn't take long for the leaf to catch fire. The sun could have shone all day without the leaf burning, but put a magnifying glass over it and the leaf will be burnt to ashes.

What would it look like for you to live a life of selfless devotion through which the power of God's love is made known? It will mean giving up on status and certain definitions of success. At first this will feel like losing everything. Yet, this loss will be our greatest gain as the love of God flows through our lives. God's call makes us a part of something larger and greater than we could ever have imagined.

CHAPTER EIGHT

Shepherds at the Manger: Unlikely Preachers

Before the birth of her son, Mary sang about God lifting up the lowly through Jesus. Like a prophet she proclaimed God's intervention on behalf of people on the margins. Yet, even Mary might have been surprised at the way this prophecy was so quickly fulfilled, when shepherds, not the mayor and first lady of Bethlehem, came to see her newborn baby in that bovine maternity ward.

Luke is the Gospel writer who includes the shepherds in the story of Jesus' birth. The shepherds are the first people outside of Jesus' family to know of his birth and the first ones to start spreading the word that the Savior is born. Luke doesn't say why God chose shepherds for these important firsts.

He doesn't have to, because when you look at the story of Jesus' ministry, especially as it's told by Luke, it's easy to see how this choice of the shepherds fits into the larger pattern of the way Jesus operates. In Luke, Jesus prioritizes the poor over the powerful, the working class over the wealthy, and the despised over the popular.

Real Shepherds

When you think of a shepherd, perhaps your mind goes back to a Christmas pageant with young children dressed up in bathrobes or old choir robes a couple of sizes too big. They're holding cardboard staffs and keeping watch over plywood sheep.

If you are from a rural area, then sheep may be a familiar sight to you, but probably not shepherds. Today, most American farmers keep sheep in large fields protected by electric fences. A farmer may have a rifle handy to take care of any predators that sneak under the fence, but in 2019 most farmers go to bed in the farmhouse each evening and then check on the sheep in the morning. They don't keep watch over the flocks by night. Some parts of the world, though, still have truly nomadic shepherds who sleep in the fields with their sheep.

Wil got to see a real shepherd in action during a bus tour of the Scottish Highlands where free-range herding is the norm as it was in ancient Palestine. The bus driver came to a stop as a shepherd led several hundred sheep across the road. Without fences confining each flock to someone's private property, shepherds move the sheep from field to field looking for pastures on which to graze. They learn to negotiate with other shepherds and landowners who do not want the sheep on their land.

As the tour guide described the shepherding practices of the Highlands, this particular shepherd approached the bus angrily and began telling the driver that he should have allowed more space for the sheep to cross the road. The nearest sheep was at least fifty meters (they use metric in the UK) from the bus, but this was still far too close for the shepherd. Thankfully, some of the more colorful language the shepherd used to express his displeasure was obscured by his Scottish accent (nearly unintelligible to American ears). The embarrassed guide looked at the tour group and summarized the scene by saying, "The shepherd was unhappy."

Were the shepherds who came to see baby Jesus like the shepherd in the Scottish Highlands? There's no way to know for sure, but it's possible. Shepherds in the ancient world worked hard to keep their flocks fed, safe, and together. They would have been tough men, accustomed to confrontation, a lot more like cowboys than the gentle figures we see in paintings hanging in church basements.

Working third shift

Luke says that the shepherds were watching the flock at night. There was no clocking out and going home. Tending sheep meant living with the sheep. Shepherds work nights.

During the summer between his junior and senior year of college, Paul got a job working for a shipping company. The man who interviewed him said that they had openings for first, second, or third shift. Thinking that working a real job all night was the same as staying up late at college, Paul chose third shift. He, naively, thought that this would give him mountains of free time each day of his summer break. He quickly found, however, that he was tired when he finished work at 7:30 in the morning, tired when he woke up again in the afternoon, and tired when he went back to work at night. He never got used to third shift.

Looking back, though, Paul remembers some of the men who worked with him loading trucks after midnight that summer. Two of them had day jobs but needed extra money to put their kids through school. One had lost his previous job and couldn't find work anywhere else. And one man who worked there told Paul that he worked nights, "Because I just don't fit in the daytime world."

All night they frantically lifted heavy packages from the conveyor belt and placed them on delivery trucks. Well after sunset, the July heat was still sweltering. They cussed at each other when someone picked up the wrong box. The whole time they watched out of the corner of their eyes for the sky to go from black to blue to pink. Then the drivers would show up and start the engines. When the smell of diesel mixed with sweat filled the loading dock, that meant it was finally time to go home. No one said "Goodbye" or "See you tomorrow." It was as if they all just disappeared into the emerging day.

Were the shepherds like these men with whom Paul worked the third shift: quiet, hardworking, maybe a little odd? Possibly. There could be some similarities.

Is it good news to the late night crowd?

A pastor we know did some experimenting with his sermon preparation a few years ago. He worked all week putting together his message like normal by studying the biblical text, praying, and making notes. On Thursday the sermon was complete, but by Saturday morning it was incomplete again. What happened?

On Friday night at about 11:30 p.m. he went to a Waffle House in a rougher part of town, taking his sermon notes with him. He sat in the corner booth for a couple of hours drinking coffee and looking over the sermon as the late night crowd came in. The longer he stayed the more he realized the message he had prepared said nothing to the people in the restaurant that night. He spent Saturday praying for God to give him new words. If it's not good news for the late-night crowd, he thought, it's not good news. Where did this pastor get such an idea? Probably by reading the Christmas story in Luke's Gospel.

When the messiah was born, God didn't announce it at the country club. Instead, God sent an angel to declare the good news to a small group of men working the night shift in an unnamed field.

Good news for all

The shepherds are just the beginning. Jesus extends this invitation and inclusion to the lowly, forgotten, and marginalized. The Gospel isn't just for well-dressed people at 11:00 on Sunday mornings. It's good news in the field at midnight. It's for everyone.

Throughout Jesus' ministry he fulfills the words his mother sang before he was born: he lifts up the lowly. Whether he's literally lifting up a child as the epitome of faith[49] or praising a poor widow for offering two small coins to the temple treasury,[50] Jesus' view of greatness is upside down. What matters most to God? In a famous parable, which happens to be about a shepherd, Jesus says that heaven has more joy over one sinner who repents than ninety-nine people who don't need to repent (or so they think).

How is it, then, that so many churches are rich while their neighbors are poor? If Jesus intentionally included the poor and social outcast, why are most churches divided along socio-economic lines? Or, more accurately, why do so few churches have the poor among their members?

---

49 Mark 10:13-16.

50 Luke 21:1-4.

Diversity within the early Christianity

In its earliest days, the church was actually known for transgressing rather than mirroring social barriers. The Gospels witness to this reality. Jesus himself was not wealthy at all and neither were his closest disciples. Yet by the time of his death, Jesus attracted a rich man named Joseph of Arimathea to his fold.[51]

The Apostle Paul's writings reflect a church that has members who have means and those who don't. This mix is far from idyllic. In his correspondence with the Corinthians, the Apostle must help the church figure out how to share life together in a way that is faithful to their new identity in Christ.[52] And the same church struggles to find unity within its diversity in other ways. This struggle leads Paul to write some of his most beautiful words, as he speaks to the Corinthians about the body of Christ and the gift of love.[53] The churches to which the Apostle writes include not only rich and poor but also slaves, free people, Jews, and Gentiles.

For the first three centuries the church was perhaps the most egalitarian community in the Mediterranean world. This kind of a group stood out in the stratified, class-based society of the day in which most organizations chose members and leaders based on wealth and status. In the early church, by contrast, anyone could rise to the office of bishop.[54]

By the fourth century, Christianity became the official religion of the Roman Empire. Constantine and subsequent

---

51 Matthew 27:57.

52 1 Corinthians 11:17-33.

53 1 Corinthians 12 & 13. We suggest that you read both chapters together in their entirety.

54 Drake, H.A., Constantine and the Bishops: The Politics of Intolerance. The Johns Hopkins University Press, 2000. 72-73.

emperors sought to use the Christian religion as a political tool for unifying the empire. As a result, the church began to look more like the larger society with its socio-economic and class divisions. By the middle ages, the church itself had become wealthy, rich in land, influence, and treasure.

One of the great callings of the church today is to once again embody the cultural and economic diversity of the earliest church. Today there are certainly churches throughout the world where people of diverse backgrounds and means worship and serve together. But there are not enough of them. We are convinced that Jesus gives us the power to overcome the divisions that exist in our culture. We've seen it happen.

Wil once pastored a church in a town where poverty was rampant. By contrast, the church's membership was mostly, though not entirely, middle and upper-middle class. While the congregation was friendly and did a lot to provide for the physical needs of their neighbors, the people who received food and clothing from the church's ministries did not feel welcome in the pews on Sunday mornings.

The leaders of the church noticed this disparity and began to ask new questions: What are the greatest needs of our community, and how is God calling us to address them? These questions helped them look beyond the symptoms toward the underlying causes of the pain in their community. It didn't take long for them to see how addiction was harming the lives of so many of their neighbors. After lots of prayer and preparation, the church launched a recovery ministry for people in the grip of chemical dependency. Within months, the diversity of the church's Sunday morning crowd was transformed. Doctors and lawyers were worshiping alongside people who lived in public housing. CEOs were becoming friends with people who worked minimum-wage jobs. It wasn't always easy, but before long most of the congregation embraced the church's new identity, not a club for people like themselves but a community that looked more like the Kingdom of God.

One church member was out in public and heard someone derogatorily refer to the congregation as "that church for those people." He responded, "No, ma'am. We aren't a church for those people. We are those people." His words became a new vision for the transformed church. We are all those people because we recognize our shared need for Jesus Christ and his grace.

Announce, invite, send

God chooses the shepherds to be the first people in the greater Bethlehem metropolitan area to learn of Jesus' birth. But God doesn't stop there. The angel not only informs the shepherds about Jesus but invites them to come be guests of the holy family, to behold the newborn king. What happens next is truly amazing. The shepherds leave the manger and go tell everyone about the newborn king.

> ***So they hurried off and found Mary and Joseph, and the baby, who was lying in the manger. When they had seen him, they spread the word concerning what had been told them about this child.***
>
> **Luke 2:16-17**

After Mary, they are the first preachers of Christmas. These shepherds are more than just recipients. They are participants in the good news.

There's a pattern here in this story about the shepherds that we would do well to notice:

- The message is announced as good news to all people.
- Those who are new are welcomed in.
- Though they are new and they probably don't have degrees in theology, these newcomers are entrusted with the first public Christmas proclamation.

Unlikely preachers

Did the shepherds start spreading the word right away? If so, maybe they woke up the whole neighborhood with their excitement. Luke says that they partied all the way home. It might have been a silent night at first, but it turned into a boisterous night of joy and celebration.

> ***The shepherds returned, glorifying and praising God for all the things they had heard and seen, which were just as they had been told.***
>
> **Luke 2:20**

Isn't it just like the God we meet in the Bible to bypass the rich and powerful, who were probably asleep when it all happened, and bring in the shepherds from the third shift? Later it will be the fishermen whom Jesus will call as his first disciples. Then, at Jesus' resurrection, God will commission the women to be the first Easter preachers. Let's consider what it would mean for us to join them in waking up the neighborhood.

Don't keep it to yourself

If you are a church-goer, ask yourself: What would it look like for your church to share the good news more broadly, receive outsiders more readily, and more fearlessly bless them to go tell others about Jesus? Our guess is it would be messy, and it would be a revolution.

Whether you are a church-goer or not, spend a moment pondering the diversity of your friends and how you react in diverse settings. Do you find yourself avoiding interactions with people of a different background? Wil claims the most diverse environment he ever experienced was high school. Since then he has discovered he must be extremely intentional about choosing to seek out diverse relationships because society will naturally funnel him into homogeneous groups. Is it time for you to intentionally seek out relationships with those who do not share your socio-economic background?

Perhaps in diverse groups, you tend to shy away from sharing your perspective on important matters because you find the education level, professional achievements, or life history of others in the room intimidating? Have you been withholding your truth from others because you believe they have no reason to listen to someone like you? It may be you are exactly the type of person from whom they need to hear.

We know this can sound overwhelming, but big things often start small. This Christmas, what is one way you could put yourself in position to have conversations with folks whose paths do not usually cross with your own?

CHAPTER NINE

Wise Men & Refugees:

The Odd Company Jesus Keeps

Of all the cultural Christmas traditions celebrated around the world, gift-giving is far and away the most well-known and widely practiced. As you may know, this tradition is often traced back to the story of the Wise Men who traveled from the East to bring gifts to Jesus as recorded in the second chapter of the Gospel of Matthew. Much has been speculated about what can be learned about Jesus by the gifts given to him by the Wise Men: gold, frankincense, and myrrh. The famous hymn, "We Three Kings," sums up the meaning of gifts succinctly by noting Jesus is "king and God and sacrifice" since gold is given to kings, frankincense is a type of incense often used in worship in the ancient world, and myrrh is a perfume employed in the first century to prepare bodies for burial. The importance of the Wise Men, however, resides not only in their gifts. The inclusion of the Wise Men in the Gospel of Matthew and the unexpected journey their visit prompts for Jesus and his family teach us equally as much.

Imagine for a moment the gifts you expect to find under the tree with your name on them next Christmas. Most likely, you already know the names of each person who will place a gift under the tree for you and the approximate monetary value of the gift. If you open a gift and discover someone spent significantly more on you than you expected, you may well respond by saying, "You shouldn't have spent so much on me" or "I can't possibly accept this."[55] The giver will then tell you why they chose to do so, either because the symbolism of the gift meant so much to them or because they got it on sale at a vastly discounted price, to convince you to keep the gift. Chances are you will respond by accepting the gift with a kind smile while secretly plotting how to do something exceedingly nice for them in return.

Now, think about what it would be like next Christmas when you gather around the tree to receive an unexpected knock on your front door from exquisitely dressed foreigners who inform you they come bearing gifts and intend to celebrate Christmas with your family. Of course, you protest and tell them they must have the wrong address, but they insist you open their gifts before they leave. Upon doing so, you see these foreigners have spent thousands upon thousands of dollars on you and your family, much more than you could begin to repay or reciprocate. You immediately begin to worry about the implications of accepting such gifts. What kind of strings are attached? What will be expected of me in return if I accept a gift like this? In all likelihood, due to these concerns, you would reject the gifts and maybe rightfully so.

Sadly, the church throughout the centuries has often ignored the implications of Mary and Joseph's acceptance on Jesus' behalf of the gifts from the Wise Men, foreigners who showed up unannounced with extremely expensive gifts. As

---

55 Unless, of course, you are a young child, in which case, chances are you will simply wildly celebrate the gift and immediately begin preparing to put it use without any concern in the world for the expense incurred by the giver – a response which ironically may be a better way to show your sincere gratitude than the more predictably muted and scripted reactions of adults.

it turns out, these gifts come with strings attached, affecting how we understand Jesus and how we follow him.

The Gift of the Wise Men

There is significant debate about the exact identity of the Wise Men. Matthew 2:1-2 states,

> ***After Jesus was born in Bethlehem in Judea, during the time of King Herod, Magi from the east came to Jerusalem and asked, 'Where is the one who has been born king of the Jews? We saw his star when it rose and have come to worship him.'***

The original Greek term used to refer to these foreign visitors as *magi,* which is often translated as Wise Men. While the Bible is scarce on details about their identity, telling us only that they resided in the East and watched the stars, some scholars today believe the Wise Men were Zoroastrian priests from the region around Persia. Zoroastrianism, which is still around in small numbers today, was one of the very few religions in the ancient world which along with Judaism believed in only one God rather than multiple Gods. Ancient Zoroastrian texts reveal Zoroastrian priests were trained in astrology as a way of dating major events by the positions of the stars. Apparently, the Magi saw something in the stars which led them to believe a new king had been born in the region around Jerusalem and they set out to bring gifts to the newborn king.

The Magi are certainly notable examples of how God was at work through Jesus in the lives of Gentiles, not just Jews. Their ways of searching the stars for truth led them to take great risks and incur great expense to honor Jesus.

In today's world, it is not uncommon for Christians to act as if the Church, and sometimes their own denomination or local church, are the only ones to whom God imparts truth. The Magi directly challenged this assertion. Their lives show how God uses even traditions outside of mainstream Christianity to witness to the truth of Jesus.

The Prince of Peace in a Violent World

We wish we could end this chapter right here. We wish the story of the Wise Men ended with "after worshiping Jesus and giving him their gifts, the Magi had a safe and uneventful journey home and lived happily ever after." Unfortunately, real life is more complex.

You may remember that as the Wise Men searched for Jesus, they stopped briefly in Jerusalem to see King Herod. Ever paranoid and power hungry, Herod waited patiently for the Wise Men to return to his palace and share the identity of the child born to be the King of the Jews with the intention of the using this information to murder Jesus and keep the designation of King of the Jews all to himself.

Matthew's Gospel tells us what happened next.

> ***And having been warned in a dream not to go back to Herod, they [the Magi] returned to their country by another route.***
>
> ***When they had gone, an angel of the Lord appeared to Joseph in a dream. 'Get up,' he said, 'take the child and his mother and escape to Egypt. Stay there until I tell you, for Herod is going to search for the child to kill him.'***
>
> ***So he got up, took the child and his mother during the night and left for Egypt, where he stayed until the death of Herod. And so was fulfilled what the Lord had said through the prophet: 'Out of Egypt I called my son.'***

When Herod realized that he had been outwitted by the Magi, he was furious, and he gave orders to kill all the boys in Bethlehem and its vicinity who were two years old and under, in accordance with the time he had learned from the Magi...

After Herod died, an angel of the Lord appeared in a dream to Joseph in Egypt and said, 'Get up, take the child and his mother and go to the land of Israel, for those who were trying to take the child's life are dead.'

So he got up, took the child and his mother and went to the land of Israel. But when he heard that Archelaus was reigning in Judea in place of his father Herod, he was afraid to go there. Having been warned in a dream, he withdrew to the district of Galilee, and he went and lived in a town called Nazareth. So was fulfilled what was said through the prophets, that he would be called a Nazarene.

Matthew 2:12-16, 19-23

Jesus' escape to Egypt and the subsequent slaughter of innocent toddlers by Herod's forces raises all sorts of troubling questions for us:

- If God warned the Wise Men in a dream to return home by another route to avoid King Herod, why didn't God warn them previously not to visit Herod in the first place so they would not tip Herod off about the birth of a new king?
- How could the good intentions of the Wise Men ultimately be used by King Herod for such evil purposes?
- Why was Jesus' life spared while many other male toddlers were brutally slaughtered? Did God not care as much about those toddlers as God cared about Jesus?
- What does Jesus' status as a refugee seeking political asylum in Egypt teach us about how the millions of refugees around our world should be treated by the countries in which they seek political asylum?

We wish we had easy answers to these questions. We do not. We do believe by considering these questions we can learn more about how to live a life of peace and compassion in a world filled with far too much violence and hostility.

Having given our personal and professional lives to the goal of making known the love and grace of Jesus, we abhor the thought of the good intentions of the Magi being used by Herod to carry out the most evil of plots. As students of history, we are not surprised.

It is no secret Christianity has often been used as a means of accomplishing morally suspect political aims. We know all too well how Emperor Constantine used Christianity in the fourth century A.D. as a strategy for unifying the Roman Empire and consolidating his power. During the age of European colonialism stretching from the fifteenth to the nineteenth centuries, European Christian missionaries often risked their lives to share the good news of the grace of Jesus Christ with foreign cultures only to have to their governments use the trust built by the missionaries to infiltrated, manipulate, enslave, and subjugate the people to whom the missionaries preached. We should note some Christian missionaries stood strongly against the colonial corruption of the Christian message while others were entirely complicit with it.

One such example of Christian missionaries risking their lives and livelihoods to protect native peoples while other Christian leaders actively promoted the destruction of native cultures comes from our Methodist ancestors in Tennessee. From 1822-1831, Methodist missionaries formed deep relationships within the Cherokee Nation resulting in many Cherokee people becoming Methodist Christians. In 1831, three Methodist missionaries along with two Presbyterian colleagues were beaten and arrested for opposing the forced removal of the Cherokee from their lands. The Tennessee Conference of the Methodist Episcopal Church, to which the Methodist missionaries belonged, refused to support the witness of the missionaries, and instead voiced its support for the right of the government to remove the Cherokee. Needless to say, Methodism lost influence among the Cherokee from that moment on, though some Methodist missionaries marched beside and resettled with the Cherokee when they were later forever forced from their lands by the Trail of Tears.[56]

One of the great mysteries of this life is the respect God showed for humanity by creating the world in such a way that humans have the free will to use even God's greatest gifts to inflict great harm. We recognize times when our best intentions can be corrupted by others for harmful purposes. Even so, we see in the story of the Magi reason to continue to strive to live faithfully and generously regardless of how others misuse or abuse our gifts.

While Herod used the Magi's efforts for harm, others have been inspired by their example of generosity and risk-taking faith to make the world a better place and to save millions of lives. Each year, non-profit organizations generate 25-40 percent of their revenue during the month of the December. These donations are used to fight human trafficking, cure cancer, provide education to impoverished children, and support a host of other noble causes. Why do people become especially generous in December around Christmas time? Because of the Magi and their legacy of their generosity. Herod used the wisdom of the Magi for harm, but today God is using the witness of the Magi for good.

---

56 McLoughlin, William G. "Cherokees and Methodists, 1824-1834." Church History. Vol 50, No. 1. Cambridge University Press. March, 1981. 44-63. JSTOR. jstor.org/stable/3166479?readnow=1&seq=1#metadata_info_tab_contents.

Why was Jesus spared?

Just as troubling as the question of how the Magi's best intentions could be used by others for harm is the question of why Jesus was spared from the slaughter while other toddlers and their families experienced unspeakable horror.

As we continue to read the Gospel accounts of Jesus' life and death on the cross, we discover Jesus was not ultimately spared from suffering. The angel's message to Joseph to flee Bethlehem merely delayed Jesus' own horrific death until a time when his suffering and death could be redemptive for the world and forever serve as a witness against violence and vengeance.

Refugees in Egypt

Jesus escaped the slaughter in Bethlehem when his parents were granted asylum as refugees in Egypt. Any first century Jew hearing this portion of the story would immediately think of how Jacob, also known as Israel, first went with his family to Egypt to escape the famine in Canaan. Later Jacob's descendants, the Hebrews, were enslaved for hundreds of years by the Egyptians and only freed after Moses led them out of Egypt across the Red Sea.

Many scholars note Jesus' time in Egypt marks him as a second Moses. Just as Moses came to lead the people out of Egypt to freedom in the Promised Land, Jesus came out of Egypt and returned to the Promised Land to free the people from their sins.

Few scholars have spent significant energy articulating the meaning of this episode for the land of Egypt. In the Bible, the word "Egypt" is usually used in the negative context. Egypt is home of the slave owners. Egypt is a place of oppression and humiliation. Egypt is evil.

In the greatest moment of peril in Jesus' early life, however, an angel instructs his family to go to Egypt and Egypt receives them. We imagine life as refugees in the foreign Egyptian culture was arduous and stressful. Even so, the Bible contains no mention of Jesus' family being mistreated or abused. In the story of Jesus' family, Egypt plays the role it was originally intended to play in the story of Jacob's family as a place of refuge from danger.

We find in this story the redemption of Egypt. A land intended to be a place of refuge which became a citadel of slavery now has the chance to redeem itself by sheltering the most precious and vulnerable refugee the world has ever known: God in the flesh, Jesus, son of Mary.

Perhaps you know what it is to need redemption. You can look back on your life and see how you used your resources and talents for selfish purposes. You can see how you turned a blind eye to those who needed your help and protection. We all have these types of regrets. For some of us they are a small part of our stories. For others, they seem to define our stories. In either case, do not despair. God gave Egypt, the land of slavery, the opportunity to redeem itself by sheltering Jesus. God will give you an opportunity to experience redemption and use your talents and resources to protect and restore those in need. So be ready and watching for your chance. You never know when it will appear.

Refugees today

One of the ways we can all help protect those in great need is by lifting up the humanitarian needs of the millions of refugees around the world. Unfortunately, in modern day America the basic humanitarian needs of refugees have become an overly politicized and polarizing issue. We acknowledge we do not have a perfect political solution for the refugee crises of the twenty-first century. Still, when we look upon the faces of refugees, we cannot help but see the face of Jesus who became a refugee at such a young and vulnerable age.

In response to refugees bussed from the border through their town, members of Wil's church started an outreach ministry to supply basic clothing and nutritional needs to the refugees who traveled through. One member of Wil's church, worried the ministry demonstrated an attempt to promote a partisan political agenda regarding immigration, questioned whether the ministry should continue. However, when this church member saw first-hand children traveling in January to the northern United States without winter coats, he was moved to give of his own resources for this ministry.

Refugees need their basic needs met and they need justice, the opportunity to settle in a land where they can safely make a living and raise a family. While we do not know the perfect solutions for how refugees should be screened and resettled, we do know if we fail to approach their plight with compassion, the solutions will never be found and we will fail to honor the refugee child from Egypt who grew to become Jesus of Nazareth.

The best laid plans

Upon learning of Herod's death, Joseph planned to return to Bethlehem, the location of Jesus' birth and, most likely, the home of Joseph's family. When he heard Herod's son, Archelaus, was ruling in Herod's place, Joseph instead moved the family north to Nazareth, most likely the home of Mary's family, where Jesus could grow up in relative safety and obscurity.

In our present day, many people present Jesus as someone you should follow to make your life easier. We are not so sure. Jesus ended up making Mary and Joseph's lives significantly more difficult. Thanks to Jesus, Mary and Joseph had to repeatedly change their plans and their means for providing for their family. They also were given the chance to witness and participate in the work of God in a way no one else ever has.

If you are beginning to consider following Jesus, please heed this warning. Do not give your life to Jesus to make your life easier. It will not work. On the other hand, if you desire to know the greatest depths of love, to learn to look upon others with the greatest heights of compassion, and to cling to a hope the greatest powers of evil cannot take from you, then follow Jesus. Like the Magi, you will find God leading you home by a different route.

CHAPTER TEN

Angels All Around

God's messengers

Nearly every major character in the Christmas story (besides the baby Jesus) receives significant guidance from an angel.[57] The word "angel" is used around twenty times in Matthew and twenty-six times in Luke. Angels are everywhere in our celebration of Christmas. They are found in nearly all of the most-loved Christmas hymns and ubiquitous in Christmas cards and decorations. It's fair to say that the Christmas angels have captured our collective attention.

The English word "angel" comes from the Greek *angelos*, which means "messenger." Sometimes when the New Testament writers use the word *angelos* they simply mean a person who delivers a message, like a mail carrier or news anchor. Most of the time, however, *angelos* refers to some kind of heavenly being, and an encounter with these beings is a supernatural experience.

What do angels look like? How do they sound? The Bible is vague on these details. We never get a nuanced description

---

57 Zechariah's wife, Elizabeth, does not have an encounter with an angel, though the angel's announcement to Zechariah is certainly a word for her as well (Luke 1:11-20). And it's debatable as to whether or not the Wise Men heard from an angel in the dream that warned them not to return to Herod (Matthew 2:12).

of an angel's physical appearance. Angels sometimes seem to have human features, and in a few places, they are simply called "men." For example, at the beginning of the book of Acts, when Jesus ascends into heaven, two angels show up to help the disciples understand what has just taken place:

> ***They were looking intently up into the sky as [Jesus] was going, when suddenly two men dressed in white stood beside them. 'Men of Galilee,' they said, 'why do you stand here looking into the sky? This same Jesus, who has been taken from you into heaven, will come back in the same way you have seen him go into heaven.'***
>
> **Acts 1:10-11**

Other times, the appearance of an angel seems to be so overwhelming that it terrifies people. This is certainly the case when the angel appears at the tomb of Jesus in Matthew's story of the resurrection:

> ***...an angel of the Lord came down from heaven and, going to the tomb, rolled back the stone and sat on it. His appearance was like lightning, and his clothes were as white as snow. The guards were so afraid of him that they shook and became like dead men.***
>
> **Matthew 28:2-4**

What should we make of all of this talk about angels? Do they still appear today?

Have you ever seen an angel?

We have been pastors long enough to hear a few stories that defy explanation. Or at the very least, stories like these make us wonder.

There's the woman who was awakened by the ringing of a

bell in her bedroom in the early morning when a dear friend, hundreds of miles away, died following a lengthy illness. "I was aware that my friend might die any day," she said. "But when I heard the bell just before sunrise, I knew. I knew she was gone. The strange thing is that I don't have any bells in my house."

We have a friend who was miraculously rescued from an industrial plant fire by a figure whom no one saw enter or leave the facility.

And on several occasions, people in our congregations have told us about mysterious visitors in their hospital rooms, people they've never seen before or since, who offered words of comfort before surgery or after a heart attack. In one case, a woman was visited by a man who said nothing, only putting his hand on her shoulder. She doesn't remember seeing him leave the room. But soon after he was gone, she recovered fully from her illness.

Could these people have been dreaming? Might they be remembering what they want to instead of what actually happened? Of course.

But these are not people who are prone to exaggeration. These are trustworthy people, not attention-seekers. While we could always find ways to be skeptical, we choose to be open to the possibility that God works in ways that are beyond our understanding. Who are we to place limits on what God can do?

Matthew: Dreaming of angels

If the people who shared these experiences with us were dreaming of angels, then they are in good company. The first angel mentioned in the New Testament appears in a dream to a carpenter named Joseph. After learning that his fiancée

Mary is pregnant, and knowing that the child is not his, Joseph decides to end the engagement quietly. God intervenes through an angel:

> ***But after he had considered this, an angel of the Lord appeared to him in a dream and said, 'Joseph son of David, do not be afraid to take Mary home as your wife, because what is conceived in her is from the Holy Spirit.'***
>
> **Matthew 1:20**

What did the angel look like? Was it the same angel each time? Matthew doesn't tell us. Though Matthew says that the angel appeared, we only read about what was said, not what Joseph saw. The angel speaks to Joseph three more times in Matthew's Christmas story, each time in a dream.[58]

In the Old Testament book of Genesis, we meet another Joseph. Like the adopted father of Jesus, this Joseph receives communication from God through dreams. As a boy, Joseph dreams of rising to prominence over his older brothers (Genesis 37:5-11). Joseph is also able to discern the voice of God in the dreams of others. He correctly interprets the dreams of fellow prisoners and for Pharaoh.[59]

There are plenty of differences, of course, between the two Josephs. Most notably, the Joseph in Genesis interprets his own dreams and those of others rather than hearing directly from an angel. But the similarities in the stories should remind us that God may choose to reach out to people through

58 In the final message, Matthew simply says that Joseph was warned in a dream (Matthew 2:22). This language matches the warnings given to the Magi, also in dreams, which do not mention an angel. However, we feel safe including this as an angelic appearance. First, nothing in the text explicitly says that God spoke to Joseph this time without an angel. Second, it would be quite strange to interpret this final dream as not coming from an angel when the previous messages have.

59 Genesis 40 and 41.

dreams. Just because we dream it doesn't mean that it's necessarily from God. Neither, though, should we rule something out simply because it came to us in a dream.

Another Old Testament figure who receives a vision from God in a dream is Jacob, the father of Joseph. Unlike his son's dreams, Jacob's dream at Bethel does involve angels, though the angels do not speak. Instead, Jacob hears directly from God:

> ***...Taking one of the stones there, he put it under his head and lay down to sleep. He had a dream in which he saw a stairway resting on the earth, with its top reaching to heaven, and the angels of God were ascending and descending on it. There above it stood the LORD, and he said, 'I am the LORD, the God of your father Abraham and the God of Isaac. I will give you and your descendants the land on which you are lying.***
>
> **Genesis 28:11-13**

Perhaps God uses dreams to slip past our defenses. We can become experts at avoiding God, so God may choose to speak to us when we are less guarded.

Dreams are mysterious. Most of us forget our dreams as soon as the alarm clock goes off, but we occasionally remember the most startling ones. Sometimes dreams put us in touch with our worst fears. Other times, a dream might be a way that our mind confronts us with a truth we've been avoiding during our waking hours. And lots of times dreams are just random as our unconscious brain sifts through images and memories, causing some truly weird connections (your first-grade teacher is all of a sudden taking you skydiving in an airplane piloted by the waitress who served you dinner last night).

Are angelic encounters real or imagined? Well, maybe they can be both real and imagined. Why would a word from God given to our imagination be any less a word from God? This is risky. There are limits, of course. We cannot justify selfish or godless acts by claiming that an angel told us it was okay. But, again, neither can we limit God. The Holy Spirit is free to communicate with us and is not constrained by our rules.

Luke: Fear not

In Luke's Christmas story, angels appear to people while they are awake. Whenever they show up, their presence and the news they deliver is frightening to those who receive it.

When Zechariah sees the angel Gabriel in the temple, Luke says he was "startled and gripped with fear" (Luke 1:12). Several verses later Gabriel goes to Mary and his presence alarms her, causing her to be "greatly troubled" (Luke 1:29). Luke also says that when the shepherds saw the angel standing in the middle of their field, they were just plain scared. The New International Version translates their fear as "terrified." Perhaps you remember the King James Version, which says, "they were sore afraid" (Luke 2:9).[60]

Do not be afraid. That's the angel's message to Zechariah, Mary, and the shepherds. It is a powerful but challenging message to us today as we celebrate Christmas.

April 20th of this year, 2019, marked twenty years since the day that two young men took guns to their school, Columbine High School in Littleton, Colorado. They murdered twelve students and one teacher, and injured twenty-one other people before taking their own lives. Columbine was

60 The angel that appears to the shepherds is not called Gabriel but simply "an angel of the Lord." This doesn't necessarily mean that it's not Gabriel, though neither does Luke say that it is

not the first school-shooting, but it cast a shadow. There have been numerous copycats, and our culture has lived for two decades with the fear of having to say once again "another school-shooting."

The United States is approaching the twentieth anniversary of the terrorist attacks of September 11, 2001. Ever since that awful day we have been fearful of the next attack. America has been at war in some form for twenty years as a result of September 11th, and many of the people who have served in those armed conflicts have brought the fears of the front-lines back home. We have been slow to recognize the alarming rate of post-traumatic stress disorder among military veterans in the war on terrorism.

The fear spawned by these terrible events has also brought home for us what many people across the globe live with every day. Millions of God's children live in war zones and fear for their lives each day. In the United States, we have indeed grown accustomed to breaking news about violence. But we return pretty quickly, if a bit uneasy, to business as usual. For so much of the world, constant violence is business as usual.

During the past ten years, we have each become parents. Wil is the father of three children, and Paul has one daughter. Our children bring us joy that we never would have known how to ask for. Yet, having children in this world makes us vulnerable to fear in ways that we never imagined. The fear of violence, sickness, or random accidents can wake us up in the middle of the night.

There are a lot of things to be afraid of. And maybe the question is not whether we will be afraid. Life on earth is

---

Gabriel. It's worth pondering why Gabriel might have gone to Zechariah and Mary but not to the shepherds.

often a fearful thing. Instead, maybe the question is what kind of people will we be when we are afraid. Will acts of violence make us more violent? Will terror attacks cause us to be terrorized people? Will the fear of what might happen to our children make us inordinately anxious parents?

Of course, the angel Gabriel does not tell Zechariah or Mary not to fear violence or disease. The angel says not to be afraid of God's message and God's messenger. But this could be part of the secret to living in a scary world.

The future is uncertain, and, when we let it, that can feel like an unbearable burden. The true prisoner of fear is the one who is not open to God's intervention. What frightens human beings the most is facing the fact that our lives are beyond our control. We are capable creatures, but in the end, we are still creatures. And we cannot always make things turn out the way that they should. Though we want badly to maintain the illusion of our own sovereignty, Christmas invites us to release our grip. When we do, we can see the angel's message to us is that God has not abandoned creation.

Where heaven and earth overlap

Isn't it interesting that angels make their most powerful appearances at Jesus' birth, resurrection, and ascension? These junctures are cosmic moments. Heaven and earth are overlapping and something new is breaking open. God graciously sends messengers (angelos) to help Jesus' family and followers begin to understand what is going on.

During his ministry Jesus is God's messenger, and the angelic appearances cease almost entirely.[61] For these three

61 Angels appear during Jesus' ministry (outside his birth, resurrection, and ascension) to care for him at the end of his temptation in the desert (Matthew 4:11 and Mark 1:13), and an angel comes to strengthen Jesus in the hours before his arrest and crucifixion as he prays on the

years[62] Jesus is the place where heaven and earth overlap. At the edges of Jesus' earthly ministry, angels show up to help people move into the new age. Their words still guide us as we seek to live into the new reality that God brings in Jesus Christ.

> ***Do not be afraid... Glory to God in the highest, and on earth peace....***
>
> **Luke 2:10,14**

> ***...Why do you look for the living among the dead? He is not here; he has risen!***
>
> **Luke 24:5-6**

> ***He is not here; he has risen, just as he said... go quickly and tell his disciples: 'He has risen from the dead and is going ahead of you....'***
>
> **Matthew 28:6-7**

Angels serve to confirm God's promises to provide for us, and never to leave us or forsake us. When our world gets turned upside down, God sends angels in dreams, visions, and sometimes small voices inside our heads to show us how to live as citizens of heaven while on earth.

With the angels let us sing

In the early 1990's, Paul's home church had a tradition of presenting an outdoor live nativity during the week leading

---

Mount of Olives (Luke 22:43-44 -- the study notes in your Bible may indicate that these verses are not found in some older manuscripts of Luke).

62 We are choosing to follow the timeline implied the Gospel of John, in which Jesus' ministry spans three years. If we had only Matthew, Mark, and Luke then we would likely assume that Jesus' ministry lasted only one year.

up to Christmas. Each evening a group of volunteers would sign up to put on costumes and stand out in the cold for a few hours. Cars on the busy road in front of the church would sometimes slow down to see the display. Others would honk and shout like spring breakers as they sped by. No matter what, the job of a live nativity volunteer was to stand still. Shepherds and wise men looked straight ahead into the blinding spotlight, which was powered by a long orange extension cord. Mary and Joseph looked lovingly at the baby doll Jesus.

For this event, the church had built a life-size wooden replica of the Bethlehem stable. It was strong enough to hold the most visible member of the live nativity: the angel.

The live nativity always closed down for the year on Christmas Eve at 8:00 p.m. One year, though, the pastor (Paul's father) decided to extend the live nativity on Christmas Eve so that it could be a part of the 11:00 p.m. worship service. His vision was for the congregation to file out of the sanctuary at the close of the service and sing the final hymn in candlelight around the nativity. Not everyone was pleased with this decision, perhaps least of all those shepherds and Wise Men, who had to stand outside for a few extra hours, but they went along with it.

Around midnight, about two hundred people left their pews and went out into the cold to huddle around the live nativity and began singing "Silent Night." As they sang, their small handheld candles were lit.

High above the crowd was the angel. The part of the angel this night was played by a young woman whose husband had died a few months earlier. Only about thirty-five years old, he had struggled with chronic illness, and his death had left her to raise their three young children on her own. In addition to this loss, her oldest child had epilepsy and suffered from frequent seizures. They were facing a future filled with uncertainty.

During the final verse the shivering congregation lifted their candles into the air. The woman playing the part of the angel was moved by the singing but had no candle. So, she simply lifted both her arms to the sky. In that moment she truly became God's messenger, her life and faith witnessing to the message of Christmas.

You may remember the closing words of Silent Night:

Silent night! Holy night!
wondrous star, lend thy light;
with the angels let us sing
alleluias to our King;
Christ, the Savior, is born,
Christ, the Savior, is born!

Just then a tow truck drove by. The driver had gotten a call to come pick up a broken-down car. He had not expected to see all the people standing outside shortly after midnight on Christmas morning. When he saw the candlelight and slowed down, he could hear the singing. He saw the angel with her hands held high. Several days later he told the pastor that it looked like heaven had come down to earth.

From Heaven To Earth

We believe the message proclaimed by the angels at Christmas is the same message proclaimed by John the Baptist and Jesus in their ministries: The Kingdom of Heaven has come near. Through Jesus' birth, the forces of heaven have invaded earth never to withdraw. All the kingdoms of earth now pale in power compared to the Kingdom of the infant in the manger, the refugee child in Egypt, the man on the cross. Every person and power on earth now lives under the authority of a king who cares for all because he created all and that is good news for all.

Conclusion

The heart of Christmas is found in John 1:14: "The Word became flesh and lived among us." This verse, which almost breaks human language and theology, gives us our word "Incarnation." And Incarnation sums up all that we celebrate in this season.

In the first chapter of Genesis, God creates heaven and earth through speech. God's Word calls creation into being. A little later, the Old Testament prophets will be instruments of God's Word, which has the power to uproot things and tear them down, even to destroy, but also to build and plant.[63]

God's creative, sometimes destructive, but ultimately redemptive Word became fully human in the peasant rabbi from Nazareth, far outside the capital city. He lived a gentle life, mostly among the hardworking and the forgotten. His words could be sharp and offensive as well as tender and healing. He died a violent and humiliating death, stripped of all dignity. But rejection and cruelty did not triumph. Early on Sunday morning his grave was found empty. His closest followers, starting with the women, saw him alive. He returned to his friends, talking with them, eating with them, and teaching them.

---

63 Jeremiah 1:10.

In the letter to the Colossians, Paul makes a similar statement about Jesus and the cosmos:

> ***[He] is the image of the invisible God... For God was pleased to have all his fullness dwell in him, and through him to reconcile to himself all things, whether the things on earth or things in heaven, by making peace through his blood, shed on the cross.***
>
> **Colossians 1:15 & 19-20**

Look at Jesus, the Apostle Paul says, and you will see the fullness of the Almighty God, otherwise invisible to humanity. Where, though, do we find this image? The men and women who followed Jesus around Galilee got to see the image of the invisible God as he opened the eyes of the blind, cast out demons, and taught about the kingdom. But even the Apostle himself only barely saw Jesus in that flash of light on the road to Damascus, an encounter that temporarily took Paul's sight.[64] The Christian believers in Colossae to whom Paul wrote didn't see Jesus in person any more than we can today. And they certainly didn't have a photograph.

In the second part of John 1:14, after proclaiming that the Word became flesh, the writer says something equally puzzling: "We have seen his glory."

Who has seen Jesus? The first disciples? John himself and the Christian community to which he belonged? Yes, but has anyone else seen Jesus in his glory?

Paul must mean something else by "image," and John must have a different kind of "seeing" in mind.

At the close of Luke's Gospel, after Jesus is raised from

64 Acts 9:1-9.

the dead, he meets up with two of his disciples while they are leaving Jerusalem, and probably trying to leave the Jesus movement, on their way to a village called Emmaus.[65] But they don't recognize Jesus. To them, for most of the visit, he is a stranger. Then, this stranger sits at the supper table with them. He breaks bread and gives it to them. At that moment, Luke says, their eyes are opened, and they know who he is. It's not that they figured it out or managed to piece the evidence together. The verb is passive: their eyes were opened. God made it possible for them to see the living Jesus.

Something like what happened in that eye-opening experience has been given to us. With God's help we can see the image of the invisible God in Jesus Christ. We can behold the glory of the Word made flesh. We are given a new kind of sight. It comes by sharing in his story, through worship, fellowship, and the breaking of bread. We see him when enemies are loved, strangers are welcomed, sins are forgiven, and prodigals come home.

Life can be difficult, and faith is often hard. You can't see God in heaven, and what you see on this earth may cause you to wonder if there is a God in heaven or, if there is, whether that God cares. All we can say is look to Jesus. Look at his life, his love, his death, and his resurrection. There you will find beauty and light greater than any darkness. And we pray that you will discover that he is present with you.

Jesus came from heaven to earth to be God with us. In his life, his way of being fully human, we see what God is like because through his life, we see what pure love is like.

---

65 Luke 24:13-35.

This is how God showed his love among us: He sent his one and only Son into the world that we might live through him.

1 John 4:9

Thanks be to God!

Acknowledgements

We are thankful for family members, Sunday School teachers, pastors, and mentors who passed along their love of the Bible to us and for professors who taught us to mine Scripture's hidden depths through disciplined study.

This book would not be possible without the team at Market Square Books who believed in the need for a Christmas book which took seriously the internal record of Scripture, the questions of skeptics, and the sincere faith of billions of Christians across thousands of years. As this project developed, our publisher, Kevin Slimp, and editors, Kristin Lighter and Ken Rochelle, worked tirelessly to help us communicate our message and clarify our thinking. We were blessed to work with Rev. Glenna Manning who put her ample talents in teaching and discipleship to work crafting the accompanying study guide for small group leaders and with Tom Baker of Cobblestone Entertainment who filmed and produced the small group DVD.

In the process of writing this book, our families and churches provided us the encouragement needed to take on such a task and helped us find the time needed to finish this project. Composing this work as full-time pastors, full-time husbands, and full-time fathers helped us learn afresh for ourselves the truth of Christmas that God encounters us within, not apart from, our everyday lives and responsibilities – and for that we are forever grateful.

Other Books

from Market Square

marketsquarebooks.com

Wesleyan Grace Theology

Dr. Donald Haynes

Where Do We Go From Here?

20 United Methodist Writers

The Good Folks of Lennox Valley

Kevin Slimp

The Methodist Story
Volume I • 1703-1791

Dr. Donald Haynes

Grow Your Faith

with these books from Market Square

marketsquarebooks.com

Obvious Wisdom

Bishop Bob Farr

Shift 2.0

Phil Maynard

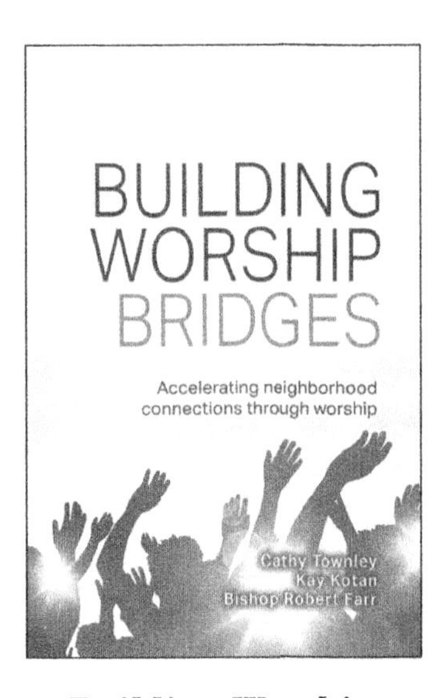

Building Worship Bridges

Cathy Townley

Get Out of That Box!

Anne Bosarge